Language Decline and Death in Africa

MULTILINGUAL MATTERS SERIES

Series Editor: Professor John Edwards,
St. Francis Xavier University, Antigonish, Nova Scotia, Canada

For more details of these or any other of our publications, please contact:
Multilingual Matters, Frankfurt Lodge, Clevedon Hall,
Victoria Road, Clevedon, BS21 7HH, England
http://www.multilingual-matters.com

MULTILINGUAL MATTERS 132
Series Editor: John Edwards

Language Decline and Death in Africa
Causes, Consequences and Challenges

Herman M. Batibo

MULTILINGUAL MATTERS LTD
Clevedon • Buffalo • Toronto

Library of Congress Cataloging in Publication Data
Batibo, Herman.
Language Decline and Death in Africa: Causes, Consequences and
Challenges/Herman M. Batibo.
Includes bibliographical references and index.
1. Sociolinguistics–Africa. 2. Language attrition–Africa. 3. Language
obsolescence–Africa. 4. Language maintenance–Africa. I. Title.
P40.45.A35B38 2005
306.44'096–dc22   2004022674

British Library Cataloguing in Publication Data
A catalogue entry for this book is available from the British Library.

ISBN 1-85359-809-7 (hbk)
ISBN 1-85359-808-9 (pbk)

Multilingual Matters Ltd
UK: Frankfurt Lodge, Clevedon Hall, Victoria Road, Clevedon BS21 7HH.
USA: UTP, 2250 Military Road, Tonawanda, NY 14150, USA.
Canada: UTP, 5201 Dufferin Street, North York, Ontario M3H 5T8, Canada.

Typeset by Special Edition.
Printed and bound in Great Britain by the Cromwell Press Ltd.

Contents

Preface

This book is based primarily on my long experience in working with the indigenous languages of eastern and southern Africa, particularly those in Tanzania and Botswana. While conducting sociolinguistic studies on the patterns of language choice and use as well as attitudes towards mother tongues and second languages, it became clear that many of the minority languages that I was investigating were seriously threatened by extinction. Consequently, I decided to focus my attention on the problems of language shift and death by looking at the causes, processes and outcomes of this trend. I also looked at case studies in other parts of Africa and beyond. What emerged in my investigation was that not only were many of the trends similar, but also the problem was much more alarming than one might have imagined, particularly in the case of Africa, where about one-third of the world's languages are found. Hence my concern over this problem became one of the motivations to write this book.

Language endangerment and death have, in recent years, become matters of great concern not only to linguists but also to politicians, ethnographers, language planners and decision-makers all over the world. The outcry is becoming louder and louder, particularly after the release of some alarming statistics, such as those of Michael Krauss, that by the turn of the century only 600 languages will remain on the face of the earth, meaning that 90% of the world's languages will have perished. The rapidly growing concern over the problem among linguists can be seen in the number of conferences which have been organised in recent years to discuss aspects of language endangerment, the inclusion of parasessions on topics of language endangerment and death in international linguistics congresses, the creation of centres all over the world for research and custody of information on the endangered languages, the provision of funds by foundations and other non-governmental organisations towards the empowerment of the endangered languages, and the recent heavy involvement of UNESCO in making consultations on how to deal with the problem of language shift and death among the minority languages.

The main aim of this book is to inform both scholars and the public about the nature and extent of the problem with regard to the African continent. The book starts by highlighting, in Chapter 1, the complex linguistic situation in Africa, which has resulted from the state of plurilingualism, and the intricate forms of language contact brought about by the many movements, migrations and inter-marriages. Then, Chapter 2 looks at the various patterns of language choice and use that have resulted from the situation, showing how some languages have become more privileged than others because of the political or socio-economic position of their speakers, while other languages are marginalised or considered of no social or economic value. However, as is shown in Chapter 3, all human languages are valuable resources as they have much to offer linguistically, culturally and artistically. Thus, there is a need to preserve linguistic diversity, just as we would wish to preserve biological and cultural diversity. Chapter 4 looks at the minority languages of Africa by discussing their characteristics, the disadvantages suffered by their speakers and the misgivings that many people tend to harbour towards these languages, thus creating an atmosphere of psychological doom for them.

Chapter 5 gives an account of the causes as well as the circumstances of language endangerment and death in Africa. It presents a country-by-country case study, highlighting the highly endangered and the extinct or nearly extinct languages. Chapter 6 considers the phenomena of language shift and death. It discusses the two major theoretical perspectives of language shift and death and how these approaches may be applied to the African situation. Chapter 7 is concerned with the maintenance of language. It looks at the different theories and guidelines which have been proposed to maintain the vitality of a language or even reverse the trend towards extinction. Finally, Chapter 8 discusses the possible measures that could be taken to empower the minority languages so as not only to resist extinction but also to offer more utilitarian value to the speakers. The last chapter also gives an account of the many organisations and centres which are helping in the development or preservation of the African languages. Since the author is aware that 'facts speak for themselves', the book makes a fair balance between the essential theoretical discussions and the presentation of facts. Examples are given from different parts of Africa as well as other parts of the world.

The book has three Appendices that summarise the language categories presented in the main text. Appendix 1 presents, in tabular form, the dominant languages of each African state. It distinguishes between the nationally dominant languages, the major areally dominant languages and the minor areally dominant languages. Appendix 2, on the other hand, presents, also in tabular form, the highly endangered and the extinct or nearly extinct languages in each African country. Finally, Appendix 3 is a synthesis of all the information contained in Appendices 1 and 2 in a numerical form. For ease of reference, the book has both subject and language indexes.

Obviously, compiling a book that deals with more than two thousand languages, spoken in more than 50 countries of Africa, is not an easy task, particularly as the sources of information are scanty and, in many cases, lacking altogether. Thus, some of the information provided in the book should be seen as tentative or speculative. However, the general observations and conclusions are, in most cases, based on substantial samples as well as on varied sources. Moreover, the author has had to grapple with a number of technical problems. Many languages are known by several names. In such cases all the alternative names have been given in the index, except where the differences involve minute phonological variations. Some languages, particularly those of Bantu origin, are spelt with a variety of prefixes, and in some literature the prefixes are dropped. We have tried as far as possible to adopt the forms commonly used by the speakers themselves or which are most frequently used in the literature. Third, because of the often scanty information mentioned above, some languages may be erroneously listed in categories to which they do not belong, particularly as it is not always clear when a language becomes completely extinct.

The book was written during my six-month sabbatical leave at the School of Oriental and African Studies (SOAS), University of London, sponsored by the Leverhulme Trust under the Endangered Languages Documentation Programme. I wish, therefore, to thank the sponsors for according me this opportunity. Here I should single out Professor Graham Furniss, Professor Peter Austin, Dr Wen-Chin Ouyang and Dr Frederike Luepke for their encouragement and inspiration. Also, I wish to express my sincere appreciation to the University of Botswana for granting me leave of absence so that I could spend the six-month sabbatical in London.

Many thanks go also to a number of colleagues who have contributed to the shaping of this book, namely Dr Akintunde Oyetade, Dr Birgit Smieja, Professor Derek Nurse and Professor Thilo Schadeberg. I wish also to thank Mrs Hazel Hudson for her editorial work on an earlier version of the book. Last, but not least, my family, particularly my wife, Mrs Eunice J. Batibo, deserve sincere gratitude for their perseverance during my long stay in London.

H.M.B.

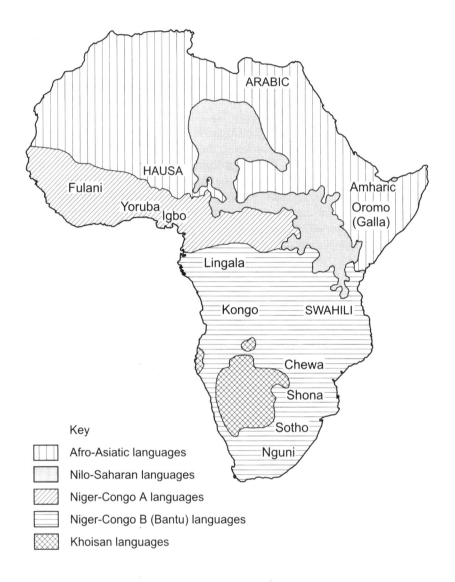

ARABIC

HAUSA

Fulani

Yoruba
Igbo

Amharic

Oromo
(Galla)

Lingala

Kongo   SWAHILI

Chewa

Shona

Key

Sotho

Afro-Asiatic languages

Nguni

Nilo-Saharan languages

Niger-Congo A languages

Niger-Congo B (Bantu) languages

Khoisan languages

Map 1 The language families of Africa. Source: Webb & Sure (2000),
reproduced by permission

Atlantic
Ocean

Indian
Ocean

Map 2 The countries and territories of Africa. Source: Webb and Sure (2000),
reproduced by permission

Chapter 1

The Languages of Africa

The Linguistic Complexity of Africa

The African continent has been described as linguistically 'distinct' (Grenoble & Whaley, 1998: 42) because of its highly complex language situation. Apart from the multitude and high concentration of languages, the patterns of language choice and use are remarkably intricate, as most people are multilingual – that is, they speak several languages – and select the language or variety of language they use according to the context. For example, a Tshivenda speaker in South Africa may speak Tshivenda to his parents but use IsiZulu to address his workmates, and then receive orders from his employer in Afrikaans. But he may use English in a bank or when talking to educated strangers, and finally use Fanagalo in a pub with colleagues. To this Tshivenda speaker, each of these languages would provide not only a communicative function but also a social role.

The sociolinguistic profile of Africa can be looked at either horizontally or vertically. Looking at it horizontally entails doing a user analysis, that is, establishing who speaks which language in order to determine the distinct language communities. This aspect of study would consider the plurilingual nature of the African continent. On the other hand, if we consider the African sociolinguistic profile vertically, we would be looking at use analysis, that is, the set of languages that members of a speech community have at their disposal, and therefore use at their discretion according to the subject matter, the personal relationships with their interlocutors, the context, the mode of communication and other circumstances and needs (Mkude, 2001: 160). In this chapter, we shall look at the horizontal profile. The vertical profile will be considered in the next chapter.

African Plurilingualism

Compared with other continents, Africa has by far the highest concentration of languages in the world. Various estimates have put the number of languages at between 2000 and 2500, accounting for at least 30% of the world languages (Coulmas, 1983; Crystal, 1997; Grimes, 2000; Heine & Nurse, 2000). The large range between the lowest and the highest figures is a reflection of the difficulties that both scholars and the African countries themselves face in deciding the number of languages in a country, and hence in the whole continent. Some of these problems are as follows.

It is often difficult to distinguish between language, dialect and dialect clusters, particularly where the speakers' opinions do not tally with those of the language researchers. For example, while the Chagga people, at the foot of Mount Kilimanjaro, consider themselves as speakers of one language, one could easily identify at least three different speech forms which are not mutually intelligible. Linguistically, therefore, one would consider them to be three languages. On the other hand, although the Sesotho, Setswana and Sepedi speakers in southern Africa see themselves as speakers of three distinct languages, their languages are mutually intelligible and linguistically could be considered as dialects of one language. This was the case before the arrival of missionaries in the 19th century, who established different orthographies for each of these varieties, thus separating them from each other. A similar situation arose in Cameroon, where Ewondo and Bulu, which are to a great extent mutually intelligible, had separate orthographies prepared by two rival missionary organisations (Pierre Alexandre, pers. comm.). Situations like these are very common in Africa. The problem is often compounded by the fact that a language may be intelligible to speakers of another language. However, such intelligibility may not be due to linguistic proximity but, rather, to one group learning the other language. This is, for example, the case of the Central Khoe languages |Gwi and ||Gana, whose speakers understand Naro, another Central Khoesan language. But such intercomprehension is because most of the |Gwi and ||Gana speakers have learnt to speak Naro.

Some of the African languages are found in dialect clusters with graded intercomprehension. Thus, the nearest varieties would be mutually intelligible, but not those at a distance from each other. It therefore becomes difficult to decide where to establish a language boundary. This is the case with many of the Khoesan languages of the Central Kalahari, which are often found in dialectal continua as their speakers traditionally live in small, scattered groups for hunting and foraging strategies. Thus, they tend to develop a continuum of dialectal differences, which do not always correspond to their geographical habitat. A typical case is that of the Eastern Khoe cluster comprising Kua, Cua, Tshwa, Shua, Deti, Chire-Chire, Kgoro, Xaise, Phaleng, Hiechware and Danisi. It has become difficult to decide how to group them into sets of languages, particularly as extensive descriptive studies of each of these clusters are still lacking.

For political reasons, most African countries do not include questions on language or ethnicity in their census surveys. So it becomes difficult to know who speaks what language or who belongs to which ethnic group. It therefore remains a matter of guesswork on the part of the language researchers. In most of the ex-British colonies, the last census reports to make reference to language and ethnicity were those published just before the countries' independences in the late 1950s.

Given that most of the African languages do not have written traditions, no standardisation has been carried out to determine language entities or which dialects fall under one orthographic system. In some cases, even where the speakers of two forms of speech recognise themselves as belonging to one language entity, they may still want to see different orthographies established to reflect the characteristics of each. This is the case with Sebirwa and Setswapong in eastern Botswana. These two are mutually intelligible, but their speakers would like to see separate orthographies established for each to ensure that neither 'swallows' the other. The establishing of two orthographies would inevitably mean the recognition of two standard language forms.

The names of some languages are known only through documentation. Some of these names may represent alternative forms of an existing language, while others may refer to languages which are no longer in existence. For example, earlier writers on South African languages included a number of Khoesan languages such as |Xam, ǂKhomani, !Ora and ||Xegwi. Such languages have since become extinct (Traill, 1995) but continue to be listed in the literature.

Finally, some speech forms cannot be called true languages as they are only created so that people who speak different languages can communicate. Such speech forms are known as 'pidgins'. An example of a pidgin is Fanagalo in southern Africa, which is spoken mainly in the mines. It is only when a pidgin becomes fully developed and has mother-tongue speakers that it is recognised as a language. In this case it is known as a 'creole'. It is difficult, at times, to decide when to consider a pidgin as a true language, as in the case of the many English-, French- and Portuguese-based pidgins in Africa.

In view of the above reasons, it has not been possible to agree on a definite figure for the number of African languages. In fact, some recent conservative estimates have come up with as few as just over 1400 (see, for example, Maho, 2004). However, most scholars would put the number at more than 2000 languages (Grimes, 2000; Heine & Nurse, 2000; Mann & Dalby, 1987).

African Language Families

Following Greenberg (1963), it is generally agreed that the African languages can be classified into four major phyla or families. These families have been designated as Niger–Congo, Afro-Asiatic, Nilo-Saharan and Khoesan.

Niger–Congo (also known as Congo-Kordofanian) is the largest of the four African language families. It stretches from the Atlantic coast in West Africa near the River Gambia across West Africa to the Indian Ocean in eastern Africa, and covers most of Africa south of the Equator. Niger–Congo comprises 10 sub-families (Table 1).

The Afro-Asiatic family, on the other hand, occupies most of what is traditionally known as the Maghreb in North Africa, including the northern parts of the Sahara, stretching east into the Abyssinian mountains down into eastern Africa. The family is known as Afro-Asiatic because some of the languages spread into the Middle East. The family has six sub-families (Table 2).

The Nilo-Saharan language family is based mainly in the Nile valley in what is now Sudan, with pockets in the Sahara and West Africa regions. There are four Nilo-Saharan language sub-families, which could also be seen as independent families (Bender, 2000: 44). The fourth sub-family has six distinct branches (Table 3).

Finally, the Khoesan languages are found mainly in southern Africa, with pockets in East and Central Africa. The Khoesan languages can be grouped into five sub-families (Table 4). (The extinct languages have been excluded from the table.)

Heine & Nurse (2000) have given estimates of the number of languages in each family. These figures are given in Table 5. Evidently, as seen above, they should be considered as broad estimates.

The multitude of languages on the African continent has also given rise to varying degrees of plurilingualism in the 55 African states and territories. The term *plurilingualism* is used in this study to denote a state of having many languages in one country or continent, whereas the term *multilingualism* is restricted to the state of a person who can speak many languages or a community whose members speak many languages. Although, if one divides the number of the African languages by the number of African states, each state would have an average of between 35 and 40 languages, the plurilingual situation is not an even one, as some countries are quasi-monolingual in indigenous languages. Such countries include Burundi, Lesotho, Rwanda, Swaziland, Cape Verde and the Seychelles. These languages are designated as quasi-monolingual as they are

Table 1 The Niger–Congo language sub-families and the countries where they are found

Sub-family	Countries where spoken	Sample languages
1 Kordofanian	Western Sudan	Koalib, Logol, Tiro, Dengebu, Tegali
2 Mande	Mali, Côte d'Ivoire, Guinea, Sierra Leone, Liberia	Manding (Bambara, Dyula, Mandinka), Susu, Kpelle, Mende, Soninke, Gban
3 Atlantic	Senegal, Gambia, Liberia, Mali, Guinea, Sierra Leone	Wolof, Fulfude, Diola, Serer, Temne, Basari, Konyagi
4 Ijoid	Nigeria	Defaka, Kalabari, Nembe, Izon, Oruma
5 Dogon	Mali, Burkina Faso	Toro, Kamba, Duleri, Bangeri, Yanda, Oru Naya
6 Kru	Côte d'Ivoire, Liberia, Burkina Faso	Kouya, Ware, Bassa, Klao, Seme
7 Gur (Voltaic)	Mali, Côte d' Ivoire, Ghana, Togo, Benin, Burkina Faso	Guma, Lobi, Gurunsi, Gan, Viemo
8 Adamawa-Ubangi	Nigeria, Cameroon, Chad, Central African Republic, Gabon, DRC, Congo Republic, Sudan	Mumunye, Nimbari, Mbum, Longuda, Gbaya, Banda, Ngbaka, Zande, Sango
9 Kwa	Côte d'Ivoire, Ghana, Togo, Benin, Nigeria	Akan, Anyi, Baule, Ga, Logba, Avatime, Ewe, Gen, Fon
10 Benue-Congo	Nigeria, Central African Republic, Cameroon, and all the countries south of the Equator	Yoruba, Igbo, Nupe, Idom, Jukun, Mambila and all the Bantu languages

Source: Based on Williamson & Blench (2000: 17–35)

Table 2 The Afro-Asiatic language sub-families and the countries where they are found

Sub-family	Countries where spoken	Sample languages
1 Berber	Algeria, Morocco, Tunisia, Libya, Egypt, Niger, Mali, Burkina Faso, Mauritania	Tashelhit, Tamazight, Tarifit, Kabyle, Tamahaq, Tamajeg, Zenaga
2 Chadic	Chad, Nigeria, Niger, Cameroon, Central African Republic	Hausa, Bade, Ngizim, Sara, Masana Kamwe, Bura, Musey
3 Egyptian	Egypt, Ethiopia	Coptic, Demotic
4 Semitic	Algeria, Morocco, Tunisia, Egypt, Libya, Sudan, Mauritania (also the Middle East)	Arabic, Hebrew, Gi'íz, Tigre, Tigrinya, Amharic
5 Cushitic	Ethiopia, Somalia, Kenya, Tanzania, Sudan, Egypt, Eritrea, Djibouti	Bedawi (Beja), Agaw, Sidamo, Afar, Oromo, Somali, Iraqw, Gorowa, Burunge, Ma'a
6 Omotic	Ethiopia	Aari, Dizi, Gamo, Kaficho, Wolaytta

Source: Based on Hayward (2000: 76–81)

not completely monolingual, given that there are pockets of speakers of other languages either from across the border or present as long-time settlers. For example, although Swaziland is inhabited mainly by the Siswati-speaking people, there are some speakers of IsiZulu and Tsonga languages from across the border. On the other hand, in some countries like Nigeria, Cameroon, the Democratic Republic of Congo, Chad, Sudan and Tanzania at least 100 languages are spoken within their borders. In fact, more than 400 languages are spoken in Nigeria. Moreover, there is significant inequality in the number of speakers per language. While major languages such as Arabic and Hausa have tens of millions of speakers, others have just a few hundred. As we shall see, this gross inequality has many sociolinguistic implications.

The incidence of plurilingualism has become more conspicuous in Africa than in most other parts of the world mainly because it has been coupled

Table 3 The Nilo-Saharan language sub-families and the countries where they are found

	Sub-family	Countries where spoken	Sample languages
1	Songhay	Niger, Mali	Terma, Dendi, Tadaksahak (as clusters)
2	Saharan	Chad, Sudan	Kanuri, Kanembu, Daza, Teda-Tubu, Zagawa, Bideyat, Berti
3	Kuliak	Uganda	Ik (Teuso), Soo, Nyari
4(a)	Maban	Chad, Sudan	Bora-Mabang, Masalit
4(b)	Fur (For)	Sudan, Djibouti	Fur, Amdang
4(c)	Central Sudanic	Cameroon, Sudan, Uganda, DRC, Chad, Central African Republic	Sar, Ngambay, Doba, Moru-Madi, Lugbara, Mangbetu, Lendu
4(d)	Berta	Sudan, Ethiopia	Berta language cluster
4(e)	Kunama	Eritrea	Kunama language cluster
4(f)	Eastern Sudanic (inluding Nilotic)	Egypt, Sudan, Uganda, Kenya, Tanzania	Nubian, Luo, Lango, Kakwa, Dinka-Nuer, Turkana, Karamojong, Datoga, Kalenjin

Source: Based on Bender (2000: 44–6)

with other forms of diversity, particularly cultural and ethnic. As a result, African plurilingualism has had a considerable impact on many political, cultural, socio-economic and educational decisions. Although most African countries have played down the realities of plurilingualism and multiculturalism, the effect remains considerable. It touches on matters of national unity, group identity, language choice (i.e. ethnic, cultural and linguistic rights) and community culture, which in turn impact on nationhood, state democracy, equality and harmonious development (Batibo, 2001a: 123).

In dealing with this reality, African countries have followed a number of options, which include the following (Batibo, 2001a):

- To remain uncommitted on the question of language policy, so as to be able to adopt pragmatic solutions depending on the prevailing

Table 4 The Khoesan language sub-families and the countries where they are found

Sub-family		Countries where spoken	Sample languages
1	Northern Khoesan	Namibia, Botswana, Angola	Ju|'hoan, ‡Hua, ‡Kx'au||'ein, !Xuu
2	Southern Khoesan	Botswana, Namibia	!Xóõ
3(a)	Central Khoesan: Khoekhoe	Namibia, Botswana, South Africa	Nama, Hai||'om, ‡Aakhoe
3(b)	Central Khoesan: Western Khoe	Botswana, Namibia, Angola, South Africa, Zambia	||Gana, |Gwi, Khwedam (||Ani, Buga, Kxoe, |Anda), Naro
3(c)	Central Khoesan: Eastern Khoe	Botswana, Zimbabwe	Kua, Shua, Tshwa (with their respective clusters)
4	East African Khoesan	Tanzania	Sandawe
5	Khoesanoid	Tanzania	Hadza

Source: Based on Gueldemann & Vossen (2000: 102)

socio-political circumstances.
- To use the ex-colonial language as the official language – and often as the national language as well – where there is no major language to serve as a national medium. Such an option is usually taken because the ex-colonial language is thought to be neutral and can be used in technical fields. Moreover, it would not be associated with any ethnic or cultural bias, and so does not benefit one group over another.
- To adopt the majority language, where such a language predominates in the country, as the national language.
- To allocate to some of the major languages certain public roles at the regional or district level.
- To accord only nominal public roles or none to the smaller languages. In fact, this is the option that most African countries have chosen.

Table 5 Repartition of the African languages in each language family

	Language family	Number of languages
1	Niger–Congo (including 500 Bantu languages)	1436
2	Afro-Asiatic	371
3	Nilo-Saharan	196
4	Khoesan	35
	Total	**2038**

Source: Heine & Nurse (2000)

Most African countries are silent or hesitant on what public roles to accord to the so-called minority languages. Such languages are frowned upon as stumbling blocks to the desired state of monolingualism, monoculturalism and national identity, which are considered to be ingredients for national unity.

These options are not mutually exclusive as some countries have combined several of them.

African Languages in Contact

Movements and migrations in Africa

In the previous section we have seen how the more than 2000 African languages can be repartitioned into four language families, each found in a geographical area. Although most of the languages are spoken in specific territories by well-defined language groups, there have been continuous movements and migrations of the speakers, thus causing contacts between the various languages and language groups. These movements were motivated by several factors, such as the search for more socio-economically sustainable environments, the lessening of demographic pressure, political strife, better grazing grounds or the urge to spread one's faith.

Historical contacts between African languages

The first contacts began many thousands of years ago when the four language families diversified into sub-families whose speakers began to spread across Africa. This brought many groups into contact. Some of the consequences of these contacts were the disappearance of certain languages due to the elimination or absorption of the speakers into the conquerors' societies. From historical records, we read about how many languages in North Africa were eliminated after the Arab conquest of the Maghreb region. All the Egyptian languages have disappeared, leaving only Coptic and Demotic, which, fortunately, have survived because of their religious functions. Also there were many Berber languages in the areas that have now become Algeria, Morocco, Tunisia and Libya. Most of these have disappeared, leaving pockets of languages and language clusters. Moreover, the arrival of the Bantu and other groups in eastern, central and southern Africa eliminated or absorbed the numerous Khoesan and pygmy languages that were spoken from southern Africa to as far north as southern Sudan. As a result, the Khoesan languages were drastically reduced in number and pushed into the arid parts of central Kalahari, with a few pockets in eastern and central Africa. Equally, many of the early Cushitic and Nilotic languages of eastern Africa were eliminated by the mighty Bantu groups more than 1500 years ago, leaving only pockets of these sub-families in eastern and central Africa.

Many of the movements and migrations were motivated by socio-economic factors. One typical example is that of the Peul or Fulfude, who have roamed across many parts of West Africa in search of grazing grounds. Equally, the Maasai have moved constantly in many parts of East Africa in search of better grazing land. Many farming groups, such as the Sukuma of Lake Victoria, have migrated as far as southern Tanzania and even northern Zambia looking for fertile land for cultivation and cattle herding. Also, trade and commerce brought many groups together. The active inter-ethnic trading activities along the eastern African coast gave support to the spread of Kiswahili in that region. Equally, the wide use of Dyula and Songhay as trading languages in many parts of West Africa helped in the spread of those languages. On the other hand, demographic pressure has been a crucial factor in group movement, particularly among the farming and pastoral communities. Politically inspired wars have been another frequent cause of migration. One example is Chaka Zulu's imperial conquest, which caused migrations as far north as East Africa. Other historical conflicts between rulers or groups have caused substantial movements. Finally, religious wars, particularly the holy wars waged by Muslim believers in North and West Africa, have also brought Arabic, the language of Islam, into conflict with other languages (Idris, 2003).

As a result of these historical contacts between the early African languages, the following situations arose:

- Where the speakers of the weaker group were conquered, either they were eliminated through genocide, in which case their language disappeared, or the language was absorbed into that of the conquerors. In such cases some remnants of the extinct language could persist in the language of the conquerors – as has been the case with the Khoesan clicks, which have remained in some of the southern Bantu languages such as IsiXhosa, IsiZulu, Siswati and Sesotho.
- Weaker groups were prevented from speaking their languages. This phenomenon is known as *language suffocation*. A typical example is the case of the Maasai in eastern Africa, who had a tradition of preventing the groups they conquered from speaking their languages for fear that they might plot against them. As a result, the restricted languages were only used in cultural activities. Thus, a number of languages in eastern Africa have experienced language suffocation. They include Akie, Sonjo, Kwavi and Aasax.
- The major or more powerful groups dominated the weaker groups to the extent that the latter were forced to learn the former's language and, eventually, to shift to it. Such cases have been common in Africa. In some cases, the dominant groups turned the weaker groups into serfs or slaves. Practices of serfdom were common in southern Africa, where the conquered groups, particularly the Khoesan-speaking groups, were made to serve the Bantu masters. This system was known as *bolantla* in southern Africa. Similar cases have been reported in West Africa. Such systems have made the weaker groups consider themselves as inferior and have, therefore, caused the abandonment of their languages and culture in favour of those of the dominant groups.
- Where the two groups had more or less equal strength, each learnt the other's language and used them for inter-ethnic communication and social interaction. This would be a case of *linguistic overlap*. Such cases were rare, since most frequently there arose what is known as *language conflict*, which occurs when two languages compete for status and roles. In fact, language inequalities were not only due to demographic differences of the speakers but also to other factors, such as socio-economic sustainability, political power, legacies of historical domination, levels of external exposure, social organisation and group dynamism.
- Where many languages were in contact, one – usually the demographically or socio-economically most dominant – would be used as a lingua franca or common medium for inter-ethnic communication. Alternatively, an artificial language was created as a compromise.

Such a means of communication usually began with gestures and simple childish word forms, which gradually developed in complexity. This is the case of pidgins, which were discussed above. There are presently many pidgin forms in Africa. According to Crystal (1997: 340), there are at least 30 pidgins in Africa, which include Cape Verde Creole (Kabuverdianu), Gambia Krio, Sierra Leone Krio, Petit-Nègre, West African Pidgin English, Cameroon Pidgin English, Ewondo Populaire, Chad Arabic Creole (Tekrur), Afrikaans Pidgin, Kiswahili Pidgin (Kisetla), Fanagalo, Town Bemba, Seychelles Creole (Seselwa) and Mauritian French Creole (Morisyen). Many of these forms have acquired elaborate grammars and lexicons, have become stable and even claim mother-tongue speakers. They are therefore fully fledged languages. Sometimes the process of pidginisation involved the influence of one language over another in such a way that the affected language lost a substantial number of its original features and in some cases adopted other features from another language. This is the case of Monokotuba, which has lost a substantial part of its original Kikongo forms. Equally, standard Kiswahili has substantially modified its original phonological and morphological structure due to the heavy influx of foreign elements, particularly from Arabic and English (Le Page, 1964).

- With the advent of the colonial powers in the later part of the 19th century following the scramble for Africa of the 1880s, African languages were brought into contact with English, French, Portuguese, Spanish and, for a time, German and Italian. However, as these European languages belonged to the rulers, they were superimposed on a linguistic situation that was already becoming complex. Moreover, the advent of colonialism was associated with the introduction of Christianity. One outcome of the new faith was the awakening of traditional cultural values, including language loyalty, as a reaction to the new spiritual outlook.

Modern contact between African languages

In modern times, movements and migrations of entire language groups have become rare. In most cases, individuals from one language group may move to settle either temporarily or permanently in another area where other language groups may be in existence. Some typical cases are described below.

- The most common movements involve people moving from their well-established zones in the rural areas into urban centres or other localities, often to look for new opportunities, paid jobs, trading or merely to settle. As a result they come into contact with other languages and may adopt the lingua franca of the area. With the growing populations in towns, industrial and mining areas, trading centres and commercial farms, a significant percentage of the people in each African country are in constant contact (Greenberg, 1971).

• Demographic pressure is still an important factor in causing migration in Africa, particularly where resources are scarce or where land is inadequate. This problem is compounded by the growing desertification in the Sahel zone and the continued drought, famine and even floods in several parts of Africa.

• There are a number of resettlement schemes, many of which are carried out by governments. These are usually implemented to allow some better or specific use of land. In Botswana, for example, many Khoesan groups have recently been moved from their traditional habitats in the Central Kalahari Game Reserve and resettled in other areas, where they are now in close contact with the Bantu-speaking groups.

• Political or ethnic conflicts in Africa have displaced many people who have had to resettle in other areas and even in other countries as refugees. This has brought them into contact with other languages. In fact, where refugee status has been prolonged, the children have grown up speaking only, or primarily, the language of the host country. The countries which have been affected by such movements include Sierra Leone, Liberia, Guinea, Somalia, Angola, the Democratic Republic of Congo, Sudan, Rwanda and Burundi.

• Although the active spread of Islam through holy wars is no longer a feature, Arabic, as the language of Islam, has continued its spread through many parts of Africa, particularly in urban areas. It is especially prominent in the Sudan (Idris, 2003) and West Africa (Childs, 2003).

To sum up this section, one may observe that, although in the past history of the African continent there have been cases of dramatic language elimination, absorption, suffocation, overlap and conflict as many groups came into contact with each other, the situation is less dramatic in modern times as people tend to move as individuals rather than as language groups. However, the historical imbalances and stereotypes have remained up to the present and, in many cases, are responsible for the present patterns of dominance, the formation of language attitudes and manifestations of language loyalty.

Language and Ethnicity in Africa

The phenomenon of plurilingualism in Africa is closely linked to that of ethnicity. Usually a language group coincides with an ethnic entity, which is defined as a group of people who believe themselves to have a common origin or ancestry, share the same social and cultural experiences, interact through the same medium and pursue largely the same socio-economic activities. Usually an ethnic group is identified by its common name, language and culture. The individual members of the group will also have names that reflect the group's practices, traditions or aspirations. Normally, an ethnic group would have a territory and a traditional ruler, a chief or, in the case of a large group, several chiefs. Often where there are several chiefs, one of them will be a paramount chief. In traditional times, chiefs were powerful as they had to hold their chieftaincies together and their subjects had to show full loyalty and allegiance.

In spite of the emergence of nation-states in Africa in the past 40 years, ethnic identities have remained strong as the members of these groups have continued to show solidarity with each other and loyalty to their institutions. Even with the weakened powers of the chiefs in most countries, there is still strong allegiance towards them, particularly among the older generations. Ethnicity remains, therefore, a major challenge to the promotion of unity in the African states. At the same time, it is a strong means of preserving linguistic and cultural identity. Language, because it is easily identifiable and is more specific, is the most conspicuous of the features that identify an ethnic group. Other features include ethnonyms, culture, socio-economic activity, totems, insignia, tattoos and artistic expression.

Summary and Conclusions

The African continent is blessed with a large number of languages, which number more than 2000. This gives an average of between 35 and 40 languages in each of the 55 African nation-states and territories. Thus, the plurilingual question is central in Africa, as it has had considerable impact on many political, cultural, socio-economic and educational decisions. Although most African countries have played down the realities of plurilingualism and multiculturalism, the effect remains considerable. It touches particularly on matters of national unity, group identity, language choice and community culture, which in turn impact on nationhood, state democracy, equality and harmonious development.

The constant contact between languages brought about by the movements and migration of peoples has given rise to language competition, overlap and conflict, which in turn have created complex dominance patterns and linguistic marginalisation. The challenges of plurilingualism in Africa have been compounded by the incidence of ethnicity, in which members of a language group are also members of an ethnic entity. Such ethnic entities have tended to be highly cohesive, propelled by their linguistic and cultural identity.

As rightly pointed out by Laitin (1992), the plurilingual phenomenon in Africa should be accepted as a reality by the African nations, particularly by politicians and language planners. The traditional European model of imposing monolingualism and monoculturalism, as used to create the states of Britain, France and Spain – where English, French and Spanish, respectively, were imposed at the expense of the smaller languages – cannot be used successfully in most of the African countries. In fact, the current upsurge of once marginalised languages in countries like Ethiopia, Sudan and Botswana, and to a lesser extent in a number of other African countries where a majority language dominates, serves as a lesson that a new model is needed where attention is paid to all languages. Hence, the plurilingual models cherished by countries such as Canada, Switzerland and Belgium should be those pursued so as to arrive at one equitable and more democratic approach to the language issues.

Chapter 2
Patterns of Language Use in Africa

The Complexity of Language Use

It is often observed, particularly by Westerners, that Africans are good at languages and that they usually speak a good number of them. The fact that Africans speak several languages is not necessarily because they are linguistically gifted but rather because they are often exposed to many languages. Monolingualism, that is, knowledge of only one language, is rare as individuals are often exposed to at least one neighbouring language or the major language of the area apart from their mother tongue. A typical example is provided by Barton's (1980) findings in the Ilala Ward of Dar es Salaam, according to which only 10.9% of the residents were monolingual. The rest were bilingual (50.0%), trilingual (33.4), quadrilingual (5.6%) or quinqualingual or more (0.8%).

In this chapter we shall see how most African people make use of the several languages or varieties of language that they know and the situations and variables which determine such choices. Such a discussion will be, in many parts, superficial given the complex nature of language use in African countries. In fact, each country has its own unique socio-linguistic ecosystem depending on its history and its patterns of language use. Even in one country, many variations may exist depending on regional, national or areal peculiarities. The discussion here will, therefore, present the most general scenario of the pattern of language use in Africa as a whole.

The language pattern in most African countries has generally been described as 'trifocal', involving three languages in a triglossic, that is, a three-tier, structure (Abdulaziz-Mkilifi, 1978). A *triglossic structure*, illustrated in Figure 1, results from the phenomenon of *triglossia*, in which three languages are spoken by the same community, each with a distinct and complementary role. Usually the language at the top of the structure is a highly developed medium used in all high-level official dealings like international relations, diplomacy, government business, justice, and technical domains such as higher education, science and technology. This would

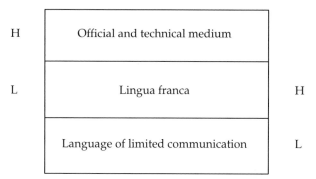

Figure 1 A triglossic structure model

normally be designated with an 'H' (high) code, which is the most prestigious code. The language at the middle level is usually a widely used
language or lingua franca that serves as an inter-ethnic medium. It is used
extensively as a public means of communication in domains such as political rallies, social services, local trade and commerce, local administration,
primary courts and popular mass media. This language would normally
be considered as 'L' (low) in relation to the H above it, but is, on the other
hand, regarded as H in relation to the language below it. The language at
the lowest level of the structure is usually a language of limited communication, often not, or not sufficiently, codified and serves within the confines
of the speakers for intra-ethnic communication, family interaction and
cultural expression. It might also be used in some village activities, such as
co-operative enterprises, customary courts or pre-school education. Such a
language, also known as a minority language, is considered as L in relation
to the one above it. In fact, the triglossic structure could be looked at as
a doubly overlapping *diglossic structure*, involving a relationship of two
languages at two levels.

Many countries in Africa have developed a triglossic structure in their
patterns of language use (Figure 2). Usually, at the top we find an ex-colonial
language – English, French or Portuguese – holding official status and used
as the language of higher education (in some cases of the entire educational system), science and technology and official Government business.
Such a language tends to monopolise all the secondary or high-level domains
and is therefore the most prestigious. Then, at the middle level we find a
major indigenous language serving as a lingua franca. Such a language
would normally be demographically dominant and socio-economically
prestigious. Last, at the lowest level we find a minority language, which
normally has few speakers and is socio-economically marginalised.

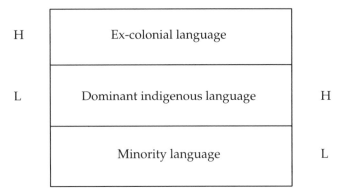

Figure 2 Typical triglossic structure of language use in an African country

Clearly, the patterns of language use in Africa are much more complex than this model would suggest.

Many African people, particularly those with an education, have three languages in their repertoire, namely an ex-colonial language, an indigenous lingua franca or other major language, and their mother tongue. Many, however, know one or two more languages. These other languages may have been learnt from neighbours, by living in another area, through marriage or by association with speakers of other languages. They would be used mainly when there is contact with the speakers and where a special form of relationship is to be expressed.

Strictly speaking, application of the concept of triglossia to African countries is not wholly realistic. This is because most do not constitute homogeneous linguistic entities where three types of language are accorded different, but complementary, roles. In most cases the triglossic phenomenon tends to be limited to individuals or certain groups of people.

Although a triglossic model presupposes a strict division of domains between languages, there is often an overlap in strategies of language choice depending on the level of technicality of the subject matter, the nature of the relationship between the speakers, the mode of expression, the context of discourse and other circumstances. For example, a woman trader in the Lagos market may choose to address her client in standard Yoruba, dialectal Yoruba, Pidgin English or, if she is educated enough, Standard English. On the other hand, a teller in a Windhoek bank who knows the customer at the counter may conduct the transaction in Otjiherero (their common ethnic language), Afrikaans (the usual lingua franca in Windhoek) or English (the country's official language).

The ex-colonial language is usually the privileged non-indigenous language, but other international languages may also be used in certain domains or by a limited number of people. This is the case with English in Cameroon, Mozambique, Mauritius, Rwanda and Burundi because of their association with neighbouring countries where English is the ex-colonial language. Similarly, in West Africa a number of countries which were English colonies have to some degree adopted French because their neighbours are francophone. This is the situation in Gambia and, to some extent, Ghana. Moreover, although Afrikaans is generally considered an African language, it has a unique position in southern Africa in view of its history and socio-economic status.

Last, there are countries like Mali, Burkina Faso, Eritrea, Senegal, Djibouti and Niger that border the Arab world or have special contacts with it. In such countries the presence and impact of Arabic is enormous as, apart from being the language of a religion, Islam, it is also the language of trade and, in some areas, it serves as a lingua franca.

In spite of the above observations and the fact that each African country may have other, unique, language patterns, we can generally consider the trifocal model as basic in most African countries. In the following pages we shall examine each of the three categories, namely, ex-colonial languages, the dominant indigenous languages and the minority languages.

The ex-colonial languages

Africa was colonised mainly by three powers, Britain, France and Portugal. (Here we shall pay less attention to Italy, Germany, Belgium and Spain, whose impact on Africa was minimal). The period of colonial rule lasted for 50 to 80 years, between the Heligoland Treaty in 1890 and the time of independence, which for most countries came in the early 1960s. During this period each power introduced its language to facilitate administration and education. Such a language became not only prestigious but also associated with education, paid jobs and a Western lifestyle. While the British with their system of indirect rule favoured the use of local languages – particularly the dominant languages – in local administration, lower education and normal socio-economic life, the French and the Portuguese adopted a policy of assimilation, in which French and Portuguese were used in all public life, including local government and every level of education. Even the elementary textbooks were imported from the cosmopolitan centres. So it is reported that passages such as 'Our ancestors the Gauls were strong and tall, and had blond hair' were commonly recited in French-speaking primary schools in Africa.

Because of the two different types of colonial policy, the dominant languages that served as linguae francae in the British colonies were given more roles and had a better chance of being used more extensively in various sectors of administration and education (including local government, native authority, customary law, lower primary education and inter-ethnic communication) than the dominant languages in regions of French or Portuguese rule.

After gaining independence between the late 1950s and the early 1960s, many African countries adopted the ex-colonial language as their official language. These languages were also used in all national domains, even where an acceptable or widely used lingua franca existed. Some of the reasons advanced for taking that decision were that the ex-colonial language was neutral as it was not associated with any ethnicity, and that it was already developed to deal with formal or technical discourse. Moreover, the ex-colonial language was seen as a vehicle of modernisation and technological advancement and as a link with the developed world, as well as a means of social promotion and access to white-collar jobs. Also, the ex-colonial language was found by the new ruling elite to be an effective tool for social distinction and the maintenance of power at the expense of the masses who, in most cases, did not have the required proficiency or sophistication in its use (Webb & Sure, 2000; Wolff, 2000).

The prestige of the ex-colonial languages, particularly English, has increased in recent years due to their association with modernity, technological advancement, information flow and internationality. Thus, one reason why Tanzania has become hesitant to introduce Kiswahili as the medium of instruction in secondary and tertiary level education is the fear that such a move would further reduce the already diminished proficiency in English in the country. This is at a time when people all over the world are striving to achieve a mastery of English. Thus, the former President of Tanzania and a staunch supporter of the promotion of Kiswahili, Mwalimu Julius Nyerere, had to admit in 1984 the importance of English to world communication when he stated that 'English is the Kiswahili of the world', meaning that as Kiswahili was vital for communication among Tanzanians, so was English to the whole world. Many people in Africa, particularly the elite, have come to consider the ex-colonial languages as central to the economic and technological development of the continent.

Even at a personal level, many parents would like to see their children speak fluent English, French or Portuguese. Many of these parents would not even mind if their children had limited fluency in their own mother tongue as these languages are not associated with social advancement, job opportunities or the wider world. In fact, the equating of ex-colonial languages with socio-economic development is practised by many African leaders or ruling elites, although they would hesitate to admit it publicly. It is for this reason that many OAU (now AU) declarations and regional resolutions on the promotion of indigenous languages have been given little attention (Bamgbose, 2000).

The ex-colonial languages are also known as languages of wider communication (LWC) because of their extensive use all over the world and the association with modern technology and information flow. Six ex-colonial languages are relevant to our study: English, French, Portuguese, Spanish, German, and Italian. However, Arabic has been included as a language of wider communication for some countries where it has been adopted as a second language, as in the case of Comoro (see Appendix 3).

The dominant languages

In most African countries there are dominant languages that are not only demographically superior but also socio-economically prestigious. In most cases, such languages have also assumed the role of a lingua franca as they are spoken as a second language by a significant number of the rest of the population. These languages will be referred to in this study as *dominant languages*. The dominant languages often serve as linguae francae for inter-ethnic communication at local, national or regional levels. They are usually standardised and reasonably codified. Apart from the existence of a relatively stable orthography, they may have a comprehensively described grammar and a useful dictionary or glossary. The quantity, quality and range of documentation usually depends on the official, national or specific role that they have been accorded or, sometimes, on historical circumstances.

Depending on the country's language policy, such languages would also be used together with the ex-colonial language in some official settings, such as lower education, mass media, some sections of the judiciary and legislature, and local government. They would normally have some form of prestige either areally (in a specific area within a country), nationally (within a given country) or regionally (across national borders). They would attract second language learners from the other less prestigious languages because of the socio-economic promotion, access to wider communication and their demographic superiority.

There are three types of dominant language: those of areal, of national, and of regional importance. In the following pages we shall consider each type in turn as they are relevant to our discussion.

Languages of areal importance

There are a number of African dominant languages that play areal roles, i.e. their prestige or function extends only over a certain area within a country. In most cases, they are demographically superior to neighbouring languages, or their speakers are associated with political or socio-economic predominance in the area. Many speakers of the neighbouring languages speak them as a second language and may use them for inter-ethnic communication. These languages have remained areally based for one or other of the following reasons.

There are languages which are demographically important and have considerable areal dynamism but whose sphere of influence has not extended to the national level because of competition with other equally dominant languages in the same country. This is the case of Hausa, Yoruba and Igbo (Nigeria), Lingala, Kiswahili, Luba-Katanga and Kikongo (DRC), Umbundu, Kimbundu and Kikongo (Angola), Chibemba, Chitonga and Chinyanja (Zambia), Fuuta Jalon, Malinke and Susu (Guinea). Some of these languages play some public role within their areas of influence.

In some countries there are languages that are spoken by a sizable number of the population but which have failed to attain national status because of resistance from the speakers of the other languages or because of a lack of national effort to promote them. They therefore remain confined to a certain area of the country. This is, for example, the case of Luganda in southern Uganda, Akan in southern Ghana, Owambo in Namibia, Emakhuwa in northern Mozambique or Fang in Gabon.

There are two categories of areally dominant language: the *major areally dominant languages* (or simply *major dominant languages*) and the *minor areally dominant languages* (or simply *minor dominant languages*). The former are those which are highly prestigious and have extended their influence over a large area within a country, and the latter are those which have limited prestige but have exerted influence over neighbouring languages. An example of the first category would be the three major Nigerian languages, Hausa, Yoruba and Igbo, while an example of the second category from the same country would be languages such as Nupe, Efik, Izon and Tiv. In our survey, using the criteria of demographic numbers, socio-economic prestige, social influence or status, attraction of second-language speakers and cultural influence, we were able to identify 88 major dominant languages and 370 minor dominant languages in Africa (see Appendices 1 and 3). As we shall see, both categories have been responsible to varying degrees for causing language shift and death among the minority languages.

Languages of national importance

Some African languages play national roles because of their national importance. Owing to their incontestable position within the country, they are used extensively as a national lingua franca and are even, in some cases, officially designated to play certain national roles. Such languages, which will be referred to as *nationally dominant languages*, are usually accorded several public domains, such as administration, law, lower education, literacy activities, parliament, political activities and mass media. There are three types of nationally dominant language.

- The first type is the one where the dominant language is the sole (or almost sole) indigenous language in a country, and hence is incontestably a national medium of communication. This is the case of Kirundi (Burundi), Kabuverdianu (Cape Verde), Sesotho (Lesotho), Kinyarwanda (Rwanda), Seselwa (Seychelles), Somali (Somalia) and Siswati (Swaziland).
- The second type is where the dominant language is demographically the most predominant, making it *de facto* a national medium on the basis of the absolute majority of those who speak it. In many cases the minority groups in the country will also learn and use it as a second language. Examples of this type of dominant language are Arabic (Algeria, Morocco, Libya, Tunisia and Egypt), Malagasy (Madagascar), Morisyen (Mauritius), Setswana (Botswana), Chishona (Zimbabwe) Mossi-More (Burkina Faso), Hassaniyya (Mauritania), Wolof (Senegal) and Monokotuba (Congo Republic).
- The third category is where the dominant language may not necessarily be the majority language but where, due to some set of factors, it has become extensively used nationwide. This is the case with Kiswahili (Tanzania and Kenya), Amharic (Ethiopia), Chichewa/Chinyanja (Malawi) and Sango (Central African Republic).

The nationally dominant languages are normally characterised by their demographic superiority, socio-economic prestige, dominance or influence over other languages in the country, and by the attraction of a sizable number of second-language speakers. Often, they are highly dynamic and, depending on prevailing national policies, may be used in some or most of a country's secondary domains. In our survey we were able to identify 36 nationally dominant languages in Africa (see Appendices 1 and 3). As we shall see, the nationally dominant and the major areally dominant languages are the most devastating in causing language shift and death because of their power, charm and extent. They can easily penetrate into the primary domains.

Languages of regional importance

Some African languages have extended their influence and use across national borders. Here we must distinguish between two kinds. There are those which are not so dominant but happen to be spoken across two countries, such as Shiyeyi in Botswana and Namibia or Suba between Kenya and Tanzania. Then there are those which are regionally dominant, such as Kiswahili (spoken in Tanzania, Kenya, Uganda, southern Somalia, Rwanda, Burundi, northern Mozambique, Comoro and the Democratic Republic of Congo), Hausa (spoken in Nigeria, Niger, Chad, Benin, Burkina Faso, Togo and Ghana), Arabic (spoken in Egypt, Libya, Tunisia, Algeria, Morocco, Sudan, Mauritania, Chad, Djibouti, Somalia and Eritrea) and Fulfude (spoken in Senegal, Gambia, Guinea, Guinea-Bissau, Mali, Nigeria, Cameroon, Mauritania, Chad, the Central African Republic and Burkina Faso). It is the second category that coincides with our definition of a *regionally dominant language*. Unfortunately, such languages have not been given any visible regional status or function on the continent, although they could play a role in regional co-operation. Only Arabic has some regional role in the Maghrebian region, and it is the only language used in the AU – although it is worth noting that Kiswahili has recently been included as a working language at AU meetings.

To summarise this section, we can state that where a language is demographically important, socio-economically prestigious or functionally dynamic in an area or country, it may play an areal role either as a major or minor language; it may be nationally dominant, serving as a national lingua franca; or it may be used across several countries as a regional language.

The minority languages

The minority languages, as opposed to the dominant languages, are those which are usually spoken by few people and have no conspicuous public role. Thus, they are used within the confines of their speakers' territories. Since they have limited or no prestige or socio-economic function, they usually do not attract second-language speakers. They tend to be marginalised and are often considered by their speakers as being of no value for social or economic advancement. The speakers are forced to learn and use one of the dominant languages or the respective ex-colonial language. Such languages form the majority in most African countries. This category of language will be discussed more extensively in Chapter 4.

Most countries in Africa have at least one predominant language that serves as a lingua franca and which can be considered to be a dominant language. In our survey, 64.3% of countries fell into that category. The remaining countries had major areally dominant languages whose use

Table 6 The position of the African countries with regard to the nationally dominant and the major areally dominant languages

Dominant language type	Countries (including territories)	No. of languages	% of total
One national	Algeria, Botswana, Burkina Faso, Burundi, Canary Islands, Cape Verde, Central African Republic, Comoro Islands, Congo Republic, Djibouti, Egypt, Equatorial Guinea, Ethiopia, Guinea Bissau, Kenya, Lesotho, Libya, Madagascar, Malawi, Mali, Mauritania, Mauritius, Mayotte, Morocco, Niger, Réunion, Rwanda, São Tomé e Principe, Senegal, Seychelles, Sierra Leone, Somalia, Swaziland, Tanzania, Tunisia, Zimbabwe	36	64.3
One major areal	Gabon, Gambia	2	3.6
Two major areal	Eritrea, Mozambique, Namibia, Sudan, Togo, Uganda	6	10.7
Three major areal	Angola, Chad, Côte d'Ivoire, Guinea, Liberia, Nigeria, Zambia	7	12.5
Four major areal	Benin, Cameroon, Democratic Republic of Congo, Ghana	4	7.1
Five major areal	South Africa	1	1.8
Total		**56**	**100**

was insufficiently extensive for them to play a national role. In many cases there was more than one major areally dominant language, each having a distinct geographical location. The position of African countries with regard to the nationally dominant and major areally dominant languages is shown in Table 6. As we shall see in Chapters 5 and 6, it is the influence and attraction of these languages that is responsible for the many cases of language shift and death in the continent.

African Linguistic Dynamism

Although, as we have described, the language situation in Africa has generally remained trifocal, there are many dynamics between the ex-colonial languages, the dominant languages and the minority languages that have brought certain tendencies to the general profile. A number of factors have favoured the expansion or extended use of some languages at the expense of others. The following are the major tendencies.

In some African countries there is a tendency for the ex-colonial languages to work their way down through the social system, thus taking over some of the domains of the dominant languages. This is because of the expansion in education, with more and more young people having access to education, which is usually provided in the ex-colonial language. Once they acquire this language they can obtain a paid job, where again the ex-colonial language is extensively used. More and more young people want to live a Western lifestyle where English, French or Portuguese would be the preferred language. With the growing need to keep abreast of information technology, international information flow and modern technology, the ex-colonial languages, particularly English, are seen as vital. In contrast to this, in some countries the influence of the ex-colonial language has undergone a significant decline, mainly because of the extensive use of the dominant language. This is the case, for example, in Tanzania, where the role of English has diminished from that of a second language to that of a largely foreign language.

In many countries, the domains of the dominant languages are expanding both upwards and downwards. In expanding upwards, they are taking over some of the domains of the ex-colonial languages. Thus, the dominant languages in countries like Tanzania, Botswana, Ethiopia, Somalia and most of the Arabic-speaking countries have succeeded in extending their roles to most of the secondary domains, with the ex-colonial language retaining only the international and technical domains. This situation coincides with Josef Smied's findings (Smied, 1991: 4) concerning the roles of English in Africa. With the exception of Cameroon and Mozambique (where another ex-colonial language is in use), all those countries where the use of English has been restricted just to international communication are also countries with strong dominant languages, as these have assumed most of the national functions. Smied's findings are shown in Table 7.

On the other hand, at lower levels of the social spectrum the dominant languages have taken over many of the domains of the minority languages as they are used even in the village and the family. Various factors are responsible for this, such as expanded urbanisation and the development

Table 7 The role of English in Africa

Status	Country
National language	South Africa, Liberia
Second language	Swaziland, Lesotho, Zimbabwe, Zambia, Namibia, Malawi, Gambia, Kenya, Uganda, Nigeria, Ghana, Sierra Leone
Second/International	Cameroon, Ethiopia, Somalia, Tanzania, Botswana
International	Sudan, Egypt, Mozambique

Source: Smied (1991: 4)

of commercial centres in many countries, situations that give rise to the need for a common language. Inter-ethnic movements and interactions through trade, working places and intermarriages have promoted the use of a lingua franca to facilitate communication. In some countries smaller groups tend to depend on larger groups for a livelihood, and thus readily adopt the language used by the latter.

There is a growing tendency to marginalise the small languages as many of their roles are taken over by the bigger languages; hence their use becomes restricted to communication at family and village level and to cultural expression. In most cases, only the older people use them on a regular basis as the younger generation tend to use the ex-colonial language or the dominant language.

With the expansion of Arabic in countries which border the Arab world or where people want to associate their linguistic and cultural identity with their Muslim faith, there is a possibility of considerably more expansion of this language, hence adding to the socio-linguistic complexity of the continent.

Finally, the often overlapping roles of the ex-colonial and dominant languages on the one hand, and those of the minority and dominant languages on the other, have brought about a number of socio-linguistic phenomena in many countries. Such phenomena include continuous language conflict, extensive code-switching and code-mixing, massive borrowing from one language by another, language interference, double allegiances, inconsistent or conflicting language policies and, at times, states of indecision on the part of decision-makers. A number of these are considered in more detail in the next section.

Language Conflict as an Outcome of Language Dynamism

The outcome of the language dynamism we see in Africa will depend, to a large degree, on existing language policies, the levels at which these policies are being implemented, the influence of the various language groups and the relative impact of external forces. There seems to be an expanded form of language conflict – almost in the Darwinian sense of survival of the fittest (Darwin, 1859). In each country there is a horizontal competition as the respective languages come into contact, and there is also a scramble for roles as people have to choose which language to use in which situation or relationship. While some languages continue to increase the number of domains or functions in which they are used, hence moving upwards, others find themselves on the losing side. As a general trend, in most countries the dominant languages that are used as national means of communication seem to gain over the other languages. Thus, in many countries the roles accorded to the ex-colonial languages are diminishing progressively in favour of the dominant languages where such languages have assumed national roles. This implies too that the frequency of use as well as proficiency in the ex-colonial languages decline as well. Moreover, the dominant languages that are used as national media have gained so much status and weight that they are pushing the minority languages into a marginalised position. As a result, speakers of the latter easily lose their loyalty to their language and prefer their children to become proficient in the dominant language as it is judged to offer more socio-economic and political benefits. On the other hand, where there is no conspicuous or strong dominant language, as in the cases of Cameroon, Liberia, Côte d'Ivoire or South Africa (where Afrikaans, the privileged medium during the Apartheid period, has been downgraded to the same level as the other major languages), it is the ex-colonial language which remains the most privileged as it is considered to represent a compromise.

The continued interaction between languages at various levels has given rise to a number of phenomena:

- *Code-mixing* All over Africa there is an extensive phenomenon of code-mixing (the mixing of languages in one sentence), particularly between the dominant language and the ex-colonial language. Usually the grammar of the sentence is provided by the dominant language, the *matrix code*, while the vocabulary – particularly the technical terms – come from the ex-colonial language, the *embedded code*. The following are typical examples:

    Kiswahili/English: *Leo nataka kula* chips *na* fried chicken: 'Today, I want to eat chips and fried chicken.'

Lingala/French: *Nalingi kokende na Kinshasa*, mais *nazali na* argent *te*. 'I would like to go to Kinshasa, but I have no money.'

Code-mixing, which can be a sign of laxity or an indication of a person's lack of vocabulary in their own language, also takes place between a dominant and a minority language. In that case, the minority language usually provides the matrix form and the dominant language the embedded form.

- *Code-switching* Another widespread phenomenon is code-switching. This is the switching from one language, dialect or register to another in the course of discourse. Usually, code-switching is inter-sentential, whereas code-mixing is intra-sentential. Code-switching is practised for various reasons, the main one being the creation of distance or proximity between the interlocutors. When one meets a person one does not know, the dominant language would be used as the common language. But once the speakers know that they come from the same area, they would instinctively switch to their 'home' language. The opposite happens where people speaking in a 'home' language want to create distance between each other. Then the dominant/ lingua franca or the ex-colonial language would be used. There are other reasons for code-switching. The subject matter or context of discourse may fit another code better; both speakers might be highly proficient in both languages; or one of them might have a preference for one of the languages (Myers-Scotton, 1993).

    Code-switching is very common in Africa, particularly between the ex-colonial and dominant languages, but also between dominant and minority languages. Sometimes, it occurs between two languages of equal status as a way of meeting halfway (Calteaux, 1994).

- *Borrowing* The phenomenon of borrowing is as common in African languages as the two previous forms. Borrowing involves the adoption of a word from another language and adapting it to the phonological and morphological modes of the target language. This process is known as *nativisation*. Most of the borrowing process tends to involve technical terms, which are frequently adopted in the dominant languages, particularly where the dominant language has assumed national or official status or is used in technical areas. Most borrowing involves nouns, but sometimes verbs and even functional words may be borrowed. Borrowing also takes place between dominant and minority languages; here the minority language adopts a word denoting an unfamiliar concept from the dominant language. Sometimes in its expansion the dominant language may incorporate words from minority languages. Nurse (2000) recognises three linguistic factors in language borrowing: what has been borrowed; the socio-historical circumstances; and the mechanisms involved. The usual trend is for the weaker or less privileged languages to borrow from the more powerful or prestigious ones.

• *Linguistic interference* Last, the phenomenon of linguistic interference is very common. Interference is the result of the influence of one language, usually the mother tongue, when another is spoken or learnt. Language interference is most conspicuous when one speaks an ex-colonial language like English. The prosodic and phonological systems of the mother tongue may interfere to the extent that the diphthongs, vowel qualities or pronunciations of specific consonants are missed out or substituted by the nearest sound in the mother tongue. Hence, we talk of an African accent. But it would be wrong to generalise that all Africans speak English or French in the same way as there are clear distinctions between Nigerian, Ghanaian or Kenyan English accents, just as there are conspicuous differences between Senegalese, Guinean or Congolese French accents. Where such 'accents' have stabilised and become a particularity of a language, such forms have been recognised as a variety of English, examples being Nigerian English and South African English. One outcome of this phenomenon is that it has become common to talk of 'world Englishes'.

Summary and Conclusions

The pattern of language choice and use in Africa is highly complex. This is because most African people have several languages at their disposal which they use in different situations depending on the subject matter, their relationship with the interlocutor, the mode of communication, the context of discourse and other variables. There are also other language varieties, such as dialects and registers, from which they may choose the form that is most fitting in a given situation. However, the languages that Africans have at their disposal do not all have the same status, some being more prestigious than others. Those which are prestigious are also the ones that are used in more formal, technical or public domains. The hierarchy favours the ex-colonial languages over the dominant languages. The minority languages are at the bottom of the hierarchical structure and are, in most countries, marginalised in that they are not accorded any public function or socio-economic prestige.

The current trend is, therefore, to an expanded use of the dominant languages at the expense of the ex-colonial and minority languages. In many countries, proficiency in the ex-colonial language has markedly diminished, particularly where the dominant language has gained ground. The scramble for domains has intensified not only the phenomena of competition and conflict between languages but also the frequency of code-mixing, code-switching, borrowing and interference. As Smieja (1999) rightly observed, such cases are an indication that there is considerable dynamic interplay – or, put simply, push and pull – between languages, which may eventually result in some being overpowered. The end result of the linguistic dynamics at play in Africa will inevitably be the giving way by the weaker and less prestigious languages.

Hence, the only way the current trend of affairs can be influenced is for decision-makers not only to come up with policies that encourage the development and use of all languages at different levels, but also that these policies should be actively implemented and positive attitudes towards their own languages fostered in people. As long as speakers see some social status or socio-economic value in their languages, they will certainly wish to maintain them.

Chapter 3

African Languages as a Resource

The Different Roles and Functions of African Languages

Most Africans, like people all over the world, tend to take languages for granted, just as they do the air that we breathe or the sun that we see rise every morning in the east. This is because every society has a language which enables its members to communicate, interact and socialise. One of the important features that distinguish human beings from other animals, say dolphins and chimpanzees, is the faculty of speech with which they are endowed. We associate speech with human communication because it is its primary function and the one which is most conspicuous. Thus, in most African societies we use language, in its communicative and interactive role, to exchange greetings in the morning, to talk to our neighbours about the news of the day, to discuss our various activities and to conduct our daily affairs, as well as to meet all other communicative needs. We also use our languages in their written mode to read information from others and to keep abreast of international affairs. At the same time, we put down our ideas and wishes in writing for others to read.

African languages, like all other languages in the world, have other functions which their speakers use. The most important of these will be discussed in the remainder of this section.

Cultural transmission

Languages are vehicles through which cultural experiences are accumulated, stored and transmitted from one generation to another; hence the popular saying that language is a mirror of culture. In most African societies these cultural experiences have accumulated in three ways:

* By the long interaction between the members of the society and their milieu, which has resulted in a unique knowledge of the environment, including plants and wildlife, and has led to the accumulation of skills and tools to deal with it. Each African society has its own unique indigenous knowledge system.

- By the long interaction between the members of the society among themselves, which has given rise to the development of customs and traditions in that society. Every African society has a unique set of traditional practices which may involve complex kinship relations, stratified social structures, avoidance conditions, taboos, modes of politeness, codes of conduct, age and gender relations and so on.
- By the interaction between the members of a society and their supernatural world, which has resulted in the adoption of beliefs in supernatural powers and the special place of the deity and their ancestry in people's lives.

In this way, African societies have developed rich cultures, which are embedded and transmitted through each language. Language is therefore a central means whereby cultural experiences, both conceptual and material, are passed on either vertically from generation to generation or horizontally from one society to another. In most societies the transmission is done by way of narration of stories, fables, proverbs, idioms, sayings, riddles, songs, totems, and verbal education. The most important form of transmission is through education, whether formal or informal. Language again becomes central.

Identity

One of the crucial roles of a language is that it provides a means of self-identity, that is, the ability of one group to distinguish itself from others. Although a group may distinguish itself by its racial features, the type of dress its members wear, the food they eat, the houses they build or the group's totem, insignia, tattoos and specific practices, it is the language that distinguishes groups of people most precisely. After all, the *danshiki* and the *boubou* dresses are worn in many parts of West Africa. Equally, the *khanga* and *vitenge* wrappers are found all over East and Central Africa, as they are popular among women. Also we cannot talk specifically of one type of food eaten by only one community in any precise manner, as rice, yams, plantains, sweet potatoes, spinach, fish and beef are found all over Africa. Language is more specific as it tends to coincide with a specific ethnic group. Moreover, language not only identifies one's group but also one's place within that group, as it may distinguish one's dialect, social class, age, occupation, religion and even gender. Thus, a Kiswahili speaker from Zanzibar will know that his or her interlocutor is from Mombasa by the use of words like *moya*, instead of *moja*, for 'one' and *mtanga*, rather than *mchanga*, for 'sand'. Equally, one could guess that a speaker is a Muslim in a language like Hausa or Fulfude by the Arabic pronunciations of words of Arabic origin. Moreover, in languages where certain words are used only by members of one gender, one would know the speaker's gender from the words that are used in a given form of discourse. Thus, in Kisukuma a lady would say *naa-ka-subala*, 'I am going for a short call', while a gentleman has to say *naa-ka-tundaga*, to express the same intention.

Socialisation

Language serves as a means of socialisation. A herd of cows may pass the whole morning grazing in silence or a pride of lions may spend the whole night waiting silently for its prey. But human beings would find it difficult to stay together silently because they are social beings. They need to socialise, and language facilitates the instinct for socialisation. Imagine you are travelling in a first-class train compartment from Mombasa on the East African coast to Nairobi in central Kenya, a journey which takes approximately one day, and that you are sharing the compartment with another passenger. You will certainly find it uncomfortable just to look at him or her in silence. After greeting him or her, you might think of something else to say about the weather, the long journey ahead, the delay in departing, the state of cleanliness of the compartment and so on. Such dialogue is really not meant to communicate anything but merely to meet basic social obligations. African people are more given to such forms of socialisation than people from Western countries. In Africa, it is considered impolite to come across people in a place and pass them without a greeting, or to share a table in a restaurant with a stranger and not to say a word. In most African languages there are words for 'sitting down and chatting' or 'exchanging news'. This helps to relieve tension or loneliness.

Solidarity and cohesion

A language can be a means to foster solidarity and cohesion among its speakers. Since, as mentioned above, language is the most conspicuous and surest means of self-identity, it can easily distinguish speakers of a given language from non-speakers. The speakers feel close to each other and therefore establish a sense of belonging, solidarity and cohesion. It is interesting to note that people who come from the same African country and who share a national language feel closer to each other than those who come from a country where there is no common language. It has been observed, for example, that a Yoruba speaker who meets a Hausa speaker in London will not feel as close to him as a Tanzanian meeting another Tanzanian as both Tanzanians will speak the same indigenous language,

Kiswahili. However, while language can bring a sense of solidarity, it can also be a divisive element. Given that one can easily distinguish speakers of a language from non-speakers, and in view of the fact that speaking a particular language often coincides with ethnicity, language tends to reveal and even perpetuate ethnic divisions. Many of the ethnically motivated clashes in Africa and elsewhere are fuelled by linguistic differences. Of course, linguistic differences may not be the only cause, as the cases of Burundi and Rwanda show. In both countries the Hutu and the Tutsi speak the same language.

National allegiance

Many African nations are faced with the problem of allegiance. Citizens are often forced to choose between ethnic and national allegiances, particularly where the leaders want to use ethnicity for their own ends. This was the case of Angola with Savimbi, or the long conflicts in Sierra Leone, Liberia, Côte d'Ivoire and the Democratic Republic of Congo. In such cases there is a tendency for people to show ethnic loyalty mainly because of the sense of linguistic and cultural identity and solidarity it brings them. Hence, unity in African countries will depend heavily on how governments manage to transcend ethnic identities and loyalties to build cohesive states with a specific sense of belonging and common aspirations.

Social relations

Language can be used to mark social relations, or to establish closeness or distance between the speaker and the hearer. When a speaker wants to establish a close relationship with the hearer, he or she will switch to the 'home' dialect, the specific form shared by both speakers, or, if he/she is using a second or foreign language, he/she will switch to a shared mother tongue. Alternatively, he/she would use an informal style to indicate a relaxed relationship. If the language has familiar forms like *tu* (French for 'you', as opposed to the more formal *vous*), then such forms would be used. However, if one wants to create distance from the hearer, one would either use a standard form or a non-mother tongue, even with a person with whom one shared a mother tongue. Alternatively, one might use a formal style. Thus, in a Lomé street, a young man addressing a lady in Mina in an attempt to strike up relationship might be surprised to be answered in French as a sign that she does not want any form of acquaintance. Equally, a trader in a Casablanca shop who addresses a customer in Moroccan Arabic might be surprised to be answered in Kabyle, the common 'home' language, if the customer wanted to establish a closer relationship for some reason.

Social stratification

Language may serve to perpetuate social stratification. Usually in a socially stratified country, one sees a class or caste system in which some, usually the rulers, belong to the upper class, and some belong to the lower class, usually the working class. This social hierarchy is normally enhanced by linguistic differences. For example, in Britain, where there was marked social stratification until very recently, a member of the upper class would talk of going to the 'lavatory' and replied 'Yes, it is I' to the enquiry 'Is that you', as well as pronouncing the word 'garage' as in Norman French: garaːʒ. Whereas a person from the lower class would talk of going to the 'toilet' and responded to the same question with 'Yes, it is me', as well as pronouncing the word 'garage' in the Anglo-Saxon manner, as gɛrɪdʒ. (One should remark, however, that the boundaries between social classes in Britain have been blurred in recent years, mainly due to factors such as education, greater prosperity, the success of democracy and the influence of mass media on language use.) In Africa, social class systems were not common, except for distinctions between royal/ruling families and the ruled or common subjects and slaves or serfs. Sometimes, linguistic distinctions were involved. One example is that of the Mossi-More language of Burkina Faso (Froger, 1910, quoted by Reh, 1981: 510), in which the pronoun *nyamba* (second person plural) is used when addressing people of a higher social rank or among the ruling class or between strangers, while the pronoun *fo* is used to address people lower in the social hierarchy. Similarly in Akan society, the traditional 'royal accent' is identified with deliberate stammering and nasal articulation, which is assumed as a sign of authority and special position (Nketia, 1971). However, in most African societies social stratification is normally age-based. The old or initiated may have their own expressions, lexicon and forms not used by the young or non-initiated people. For example, Yoruba society differentiates between *o* and *e* as the second person singular to signal age and/or status difference (Wolff, 2000: 306).

A vehicle for thought and intelligence

Finally, language is important in human life as it is the basis of thought and the thinking process. It is through language that we conceptualise ideas, organise our thoughts and systematise our memory. It is often said that there is a close relationship between language, thought and intelligence (ADEA, 1996a). It is believed that our human intelligence only developed at the time of *homo grammaticus*, that is, when the faculty of speech became available to human beings.

Summary

From the foregoing points, one notes the significance of language in human life in that it is central not only to our social interactions and relationships but also in distinguishing us and enabling others to ascertain our position in society. This would explain why people with speech or hearing disabilities find it difficult to integrate and participate fully in their communities. It means that every language community has developed unique modes of using its language. At the same time, each language has been moulded in a special way to serve the needs of the community that speaks it. In this way, every language is a unique system and therefore a resource for human kind. It is because of the many unique systems in each language that we talk of linguistic diversity. And linguistic diversity, like biodiversity, is an important feature of our universe.

African Languages as Wealth and Human Heritage

The uniqueness of African languages

African languages are not only significant to the personal and social well-being of their speakers, but they are also valuable as a resource and constitute an invaluable heritage for humanity. This is because each human language has a unique linguistic inventory and rules, reflects its own cultural experience, expresses its own world view and manifests its own artistic peculiarities. Thus, taken together, all the more than 2000 African languages have an enormous wealth of linguistic, cultural, world view and artistic phenomena to offer to humankind. In the following subsections we shall discuss the salient linguistic and cultural features found in African languages.

Linguistic wealth in African languages

The African languages, taken together, show an extensive wealth of linguistic phenomena ranging from unique features of the sound systems to special rules of sentence formation. Many of the sounds which are used in African languages are either unique or rare in other human languages. The most characteristic is the set of click sounds found in the Khoesan languages. The click sounds are usually produced by making a closure in the mouth and then releasing the closure, so that air is sucked in. The mechanism involves the closure of the velum by the back of the tongue, while the front part of the tongue may take different positions, resulting in different clicks. In the Khoesan languages, clicks are used as consonants to form words. There are basically five clicks. The dental click, represented by the symbol ' | ', is produced by putting the tip of the tongue towards the teeth and then sucking in the air so as to produce a sharp hissing sound. The lateral click, represent by the symbol ' || ', is produced by placing the tip of the tongue on the alveoral ridge and then sucking air past the side of the tongue. The palato-alveolar click, represented by the symbol '≠', is produced by putting the front part of the tongue towards the alveoral ridge and then sucking in air while lowering the tongue. The post-alveolar click, represented by the symbol '!', is produced when the tip of the tongue is placed further back in the mouth against the hard palate. This sound resembles the noise made by a bottle when a cork is removed. Last, the bilabial click, represented by the symbol '⊙', is produced by pouting the two lips and sucking them inwards, as in kissing. These clicks may be accompanied by other features, such as nasalisation (air passing through the nose), voicing (vibration of the vocal cords), aspiration (puff of air) and fricativisation (friction between those parts of the vocal organs that are in contact). The possibility of using so many click combinations to form distinct consonantal segments has allowed many Khoesan languages, such as !Xóõ, Ju|'hoan and ≠Kx'au||ein, to have an extensive inventory of consonant units, amounting in some cases to over 100.

Moreover, African languages have many other sounds that are rare in human languages, with sometimes unique realisations. Such sounds include the lateral fricatives 'ɬ' and 'ɮ', which are produced by allowing the air to pass at the side of the mouth but involving significant friction of air. Related to these sounds are the lateral affricates 'tɬ' and 'tɬʰ', which are produced by blocking the air stream in the alveolar area and then allowing it to come out gradually through the side of the mouth with a certain amount of friction. Both the lateral fricatives and the lateral affricates are common in Nguni and Sotho languages. Other unique sounds include the labio-velars 'kp', 'gb' and 'ŋm'. These sounds are produced by simultaneously using two sites of articulation, namely the two lips and the back of the mouth. Such sounds are common in Niger–Congo and some Nilo-Saharan languages. In some languages, particularly those of the Gur sub-family, these sounds have the labio-alveolar varieties 'pt' and 'bd', which are produced by involving the two lips and the alveoral ridge at the same time. Further unique sounds in African languages include the laryngealised plosives and approximants 'ˀb', 'ˀd', 'ˀɟ', 'ˀw' and 'ˀj'. These are consonantal sounds whose articulation is accompanied by the sudden blockage of air in the laryngeal area (inside the Adam's apple). Such sounds are common in the Atlantic and Chadic sub-families (Ladefoged, 1964). Moreover, some African languages can make very fine distinctions, such as that between dental and alveolar sounds. This is the case with some of the Benue–Congo languages, such as Isoko and Sebirwa, which make a phonological contrast between 't̪' and 't'.

Some of the Afro-Asiatic languages, particularly those of Semitic origin, have many varieties of laryngeal and pharyngeal sounds. One unique phenomenon is the distinction between advanced and non-advanced tongue root (+/–ATR) positions, allowing two sets of vowels. Such distinctions are common in Niger–Congo and Nilo-Saharan languages, where there are often two sets of vowels (+ATR) and (–ATR). Also, as stated by Maddieson (1984), some African languages have sounds which involve unique combinations of features. Some of these unique sounds include the palatalised, breathy-voiced bilabial plosive consonants found in Igbo, the pharyngealised, voiceless dental plosive consonants in a number of Berber languages and the voiceless aspirated nasals in Kisukuma. Similarly, from a phonetic point of view, there are many types of phonation, nasalisation, velarisation, pharyngealisation and glottalisation mechanisms; these provide rich data for phonetic analysis, and hence allow linguists to learn more about human articulatory and perceptive possibilities.

Many African languages have phonological processes (that is, changes in sounds when in contact with other sounds) that have prompted the formulation of specific laws. Common among these processes is the deletion of an oral consonant in successive syllables with nasal consonants, known as the Ganda or Meinhof Law. In an example of this law, the Bantu proto-form (the form supposedly used in the ancestral language) **ŋgombe*, 'cow', has become *ŋombe*. Another common law, Dahl's Law, concerns the voicing of a consonant where two syllables with voiceless consonants follow in succession. An example is the Bantu proto-form **tatu*, 'three', which has become *datu*. The Kwanyama Law relates to the change of a pre-nasalised consonant into a simple plosive if the previous syllable also has a pre-nasalised consonant. Here an example is the Bantu proto-form **ŋgombe*, 'cow', which has become *ŋgope*. A very common law in some of the southern African languages is the change from a voiced pre-nasalised consonant to a voiceless plosive and from a voiceless pre-nasalised consonant to an aspirated voiceless plosive, known as the Sotho Law. Following this law, the Bantu proto-forms **mbula*, 'rain', and **mpala*, 'gazelle', have changed to *pula* and *phala*, respectively. Another common law, known as the Katupha Law, is the loss of aspiration in successive syllables with aspirated consonants (equivalent to Grassmann's Law in Indo-European). According to this law, where aspirated voiceless plosives are found in two successive syllables, one of the consonants will lose its aspiration; thus, a form like t^hat^hu, 'three', becomes tat^hu (Schadeberg, 1999). Moreover, there is a widespread phenomenon in Bantu languages known as *spirantisation*. This is a process in which plosives change to fricatives when followed by the high, tense vowels 'i' and 'u'. Thus, the Bantu proto-form *piti*, 'hyena', and *mbula* have become, respectively, *fisi* and *mvua* in Kiswahili, where this law operates.

Many African languages are tone languages – that is, voice pitch can be used to distinguish between words. The tone structures in a number of these languages are often complex and unique in that tone units may delete, spread or displace in, often, very complex structural conditions. It is from this complexity that new approaches to tone, such as auto-segmental phonology, have been born (Clements, 2000; Goldsmith, 1990).

At the level of word formation, many phenomena in the area of inflection, derivation and case marking are unique to African languages, such as noun classes, common in the Niger–Congo languages, the gender system, common in Afro-Asiatic, Nilo-Saharan and Khoesan languages, and the tense aspect systems, which are often complex and unique, to mention but a few phenomena. As Dimmendaal (2000: 192) rightly points out, the considerable typological diversity between African languages in the way they build up words means that these languages should 'play a major role in our conceptualisation of morphological systems'.

This is true also in the area of syntax, or sentence structure. Again, the extensive typological diversity in the way sentences are constructed in the various African language families has given rise to some unique phenomena, such as juxtaposition, consecutive constructions, serial verb systems, the centrality of verbs, the presence of ideophones as a special word category and the special types of transformation that can affect the basic sentence (Watters, 2000: 228). Some modern theoretical developments in the area of syntax are based heavily on experience with African languages. These include the cross-linguistic theories, such as relational grammar and lexical-functional grammar (Mchombo, 1993: 13ff).

In the area of oral discourse and stylistics, African languages are rich in a variety of possibilities of expression that are normally guided by the relationship or social differences between the speakers, and/or by context, circumstances and subject matter. Statements or requests are often put in an indirect manner. For example, expressed in an African language, a question like 'Don't you want to eat?' could be an invitation to a meal. No wonder Westerners sometimes find it difficult to understand Africans in their use of European languages when they employ African discourse strategies. Grice's 'cooperative principles' (Grice, 1975) are often stretched in order to bring flavour and uniqueness to discourse. Unfortunately, since many of the African languages have not yet been described, or have been only partially described, much linguistic wealth remains to be uncovered.

The cultural and artistic wealth of African languages

As Diamond (1993) rightly pointed out, every language is tied up with a specific culture, literary expression and world view. Each is the custodian of its speakers' cultural experiences, which, as we saw above, are the result of many centuries of interaction with their physical milieu, inter- and intra-ethnic contacts, and relations with the supernatural world. Hence no two language communities will have exactly the same cultural experience. This diversity of experience means also diversity in the forms of physical adaptation, in the conceptualisation of ideas, in ecological knowledge and the vision of the universe.

The existence of many language communities in Africa should not necessarily be seen as a source of linguistic or ethnic conflict (as is often thought) but rather as an important resource residing in the wealth and diversity of zoological, botanical and other indigenous knowledge, as well as in skills and methods of dealing with the physical and supernatural world (Maffi, 2001). This knowledge is often invested in people in a given community who may, as traditional healers, be knowledgeable about plants, or who may have powers to get rid of evil spirits, 'call' for rain in time of drought, prepare charms for those in need or carry out special divinations. Thus, if most languages in Africa became extinct, much of this wealth of indigenous knowledge, beliefs, concepts and skills would disappear with them. In fact, some of the traditional medicines used by some of these communities have proved to be effective in treating complex diseases such as cancer, asthma, leprosy and tuberculosis, as well as chronic cases of STD, bilharzia and anaemia (Batibo, 2001b; Crawhall, 1997). Unfortunately, it has not been easy to make a thorough documentation of all this knowledge as many of the studies carried out by linguists tend to focus on structural and lexical analysis. It is gratifying, however, to note that some recent linguistic studies have focused on documentation of the names of botanical and zoological phenomena and their socio-cultural use (see for example Brenzinger & Heine, 1995; Cole, 1995; Heine & Legère, 1995).

Each human language, through its long cultural experience, has built up a frame through which its users visualise the universe or world phenomena. A language acts as a filter through which its speakers interpret the world around them (Sapir, 1921; Whorf, 1956). It also provides support for our conceptual mechanisms. Thus, while an English speaker is able to distinguish as many as 26 colours around him, thanks to the terms available in English for each of these shades, a Kisukuma speaker will only be able to distinguish three, namely black, white and red. Although he/she may notice other colours, perception of these variations will be heavily blurred for lack of terms in the language to distinguish them clearly. On the other hand, as Kisukuma speakers are renowned herders, their language is rich in names of cattle according to colour, patterns and positions of colour and type of horns, particularities that are richly lexicalised (that is, have given rise to the creation of specific vocabulary). Such details would hardly be noticeable to an Englishman. Thus, every language has specialised in relation to the world phenomena with which its speakers are most preoccupied. In the case of Africa, all these experiences put together mean a wealth of conceptual knowledge of the universe in its different facets.

Some of the conceptual framework built through African experiences has found its way into the structural framework of the respective languages. For example, many of the Niger–Congo languages have a noun class system in which nouns are categorised according to the phenomena in the world that they represent. Although in their present state the semantic representation of the various nouns is blurred in most of these languages, it is clear that at one time a world view was involved, which captured a certain philosophical outlook (Krapf & Rebman, 1887). Thus, in general all human nouns belonged to one class, trees and plants to another, liquids and masses to another, and so on. Some African philosophers, such as Kagame (1956) and Mbiti (1969), have come up with ideas about ancient philosophical concepts in African languages, particularly those of Bantu origin. Similarly, many languages of the Afro-Asiatic, Nilo-Saharan and Khoesan families employ gender marking, but the phenomenon is not strictly sex-based as land and cattle are feminine in some languages and masculine in others (Hayward, 2000). Such a pattern would indicate the involvement of a world view. In many African languages time and space are related. For example, the Bantu particles *pa* (on), *mu* (in) and *ku* (to, towards) are used to denote location, as in Setswana *mo ntlong* (in the house), but also to indicate time, as in *mo mosong* (in the morning). There is a universal tendency to associate body parts with directions, as in the English words 'back' and 'front', and in many African languages this is even more elaborate. Some of the common terms include 'buttocks' (bottom, back), 'head of' (up, on), 'male hand/hand of eating' (right hand), 'female hand' (left hand) (Wolff, 2000). In this way, the process of grammaticalisation is common in African languages. These are just a few examples to demonstrate how rich African languages are in providing a world view, one that has resulted from centuries of experience of the world around them by the respective linguistic communities.

Moreover, African languages are rich in oral literature and artistic phenomena. Since most are written either to a limited degree or not at all, much discourse takes place through oral expression, in the form of folklore or what has come to be known as *oral literature*. Many African languages are rich in stylistic, figurative, symbolic and gestural expression. Although many of them have not cultivated formal styles and are not used in any technical discourse, they possess a wealth of culturally and socially driven communicative strategies. Such variations are often determined by age, social relations, the subject of discourse and situational context. For instance, in Wolof there is a wealth of strategies and culturally embedded modes of status manipulation in greeting exchanges (Irvine, 1974).

The most conspicuous expressive form of language in African societies is the use of figurative turns of speech. This is because figurative language facilitates the hearer's understanding and grasps the attention of an audience, persuading them to search for meaning in the discourse (Pongweni, 2000: 131). The most common forms of figurative speech are metaphor, simile and proverb, which usually describe facts in 'an impossible combination of words' (Pongweni, 2000: 132). In African languages, people tend to liken or relate objects to others. Metaphors like *kumhanya semhepo*, 'to run like the wind', in Chishona, or *mwembamba kama sindano*, 'as thin as a needle', in Kiswahili are very common and bring much flavour to discourse. Proverbs are also very widely used, particularly by the older generation, as forms that give authority to discourse. They are often seen as unchallengeable words of wisdom (Ibekwe, 1998). At meetings, proverbs are used as a guide to support decision-making. For example, a Kiswahili proverb like *wakati ukuta*, 'time is a wall' (i.e. you cannot fight against time as it is as hard as a wall) might be used to remind the old generation that things pass with time; let the young people do things their own way. Symbolism is very common in African languages and has been instrumental in creating many common expressions such as 'to be with' (for to have), 'thing of eating' (for food), 'he and his head' (for he himself), 'she has/is a belly' (for she is pregnant), 'she has relieved herself' (for she has delivered) or 'mouth of house' (for doorway). Equally, there are many instances of riddles, puzzles, idioms, euphemisms, secret languages and other forms of expression. The existence of such a wealth of expressive phenomena in African languages is presumably because of their oral nature and the highly interactive disposition of African people.

Finally, one phenomenon which is unique, but common across Africa, is the *joking relationship*, which may involve ethnic groups that were once at war or in a tense relationship, such as the Ngoni and Nyamwezi or the Haya and the Luo (all from East Africa), or could be between grandparents and grandchildren or brothers- and sisters-in-law. The jokes could range from mere calling each other names (such as the Yoruba people calling the easterners *Kobokobo* (the copper people) and the easterners calling the

Yoruba *ngbati-ngbati* (in imitation of what the Yoruba seem to be saying when they speak), to abusive forms, including making remarks about the dead at a funeral of the other party, or joking about the other's partner. Sometimes abusive jokes may be wrapped in metaphorical or sarcastic poetry, as in the case of the *Oriki* (attribution) oral poetry among the Yoruba or the special messages on the *khanga* wrappers of the eastern coast. Such a practice is, presumably, meant to ease tensions between groups, create some outlet at times of misfortune, bring about an atmosphere of closeness between members of two families united through marriage or to bridge the generation gap between the old and the young.

African Languages as Vehicles for National Development

As pointed out by Bamgbose (2000: 30), language is a powerful symbol of society, particularly if its potential is fully recognised and exploited. It can be a key contributing force towards nationhood and national development. When most of the states in Africa gained their independence between the late 1950s and the early 1960s, they realised from the outset the importance of a powerful national medium when faced with the many tasks of dismantling colonial legacies. Strong nationalistic sentiments had driven them to national emancipation. They rapidly saw the important national needs that Fishman (1971) has referred to as unification, authenticity and modernity. They needed unity of the many and diverse ethnic groups that had been permitted a certain autonomy under colonial rule, particularly in the British system of indirect rule. They wanted to establish an identity for their own sovereignties as independent states. Moreover, they aspired for development in order to be part of the modern world and also to improve the lives of their citizens. This was the most opportune moment to make full use of national linguistic resources as their national media had been used to bring about national unity, identity and development.

This process required systematic language planning, in which choices of language and their domains of use were made on strictly economic grounds in much the same way as for any other resources in the nation's economy (Fishman, 1971, 1974; Jernudd & Das Gupta, 1971: 195–6). In this way, each nation should have been looking for optimisation of the use of the national linguistic resources at the least possible cost. However, most countries took a shortcut by adopting the ex-colonial languages as the only or main national media, particularly in the official and technical areas. The explanation was partly technical – that these languages were already highly developed and internationally used – and partly political, in that they were neutral and therefore would not be associated with any ethnic resentment.

Only a few countries, including Tanzania, Ethiopia, Somalia and most of the Arabic-speaking countries, opted to develop their indigenous linguae francae to serve as national languages.

Thus, the preference for promoting the ex-colonial languages in most of the newly independent countries was not the outcome of some cost–benefit analysis but, rather, of convenience. The ex-colonial languages have continued to strengthen their positions of prestige at the expense of the indigenous languages. At the same time the use of foreign languages has adversely affected the earlier aspirations to unity, identity and development since many countries lack the essential features of nationhood and authenticity. One needs to acknowledge that all the world's developed countries have developed on the basis of their national languages, as they have adapted and integrated technology within their cultural and social values, thus reaching all the people in their countries. It is a fact that no developed country has developed on the basis of a foreign language as development involves the participation of all citizens in nation-building. It is no wonder that small countries like the Netherlands and Denmark have preserved their languages, which are used in their daily social and economic activities. Also, the fast-developing countries of Asia, such as China, Korea, Taiwan, Malaysia and Thailand, base their development strategies on the indigenous languages as this is the only way to involve the whole population in the development effort and to meaningfully bring technological advancement within the country's cultural framework.

In the case of the African countries, it is important that they undertake a thorough review of their language situation and establish policies which are consonant with their national aspirations, optimum utilisation of the national linguistic resources and the ultimate national goal. Such a goal should include not only economic development but also a truly democratic and harmonious way of life. Not all languages need to be accorded the same role or status. The positions and domains of use of each of the languages in a country could be determined by its relative demographic and socio-political position in that country. Hence, a hierarchy of language use could be established. The country that has tried to establish such a hierarchical structure is Zimbabwe (Hachipola, 1996: 4), as shown in Table 8.

Unfortunately, in most African countries language planning activities and matters of language policy are not given much attention. Many states have chosen to be pragmatic where language is concerned. As a result, the indigenous languages, as a potential national resource and an important part of the human heritage, remain unexploited and/or underdeveloped. In fact, indigenous languages should not be seen as stumbling blocks to national unity, national identity and national development, but should

Table 8 Hierarchy of language roles in Zimbabwe

Status or role	Language
Official language	English
National language	Chishona
Provincial language	Sindebele
Language of education and mass media alone	Ikalanga, Shangani, Chitonga, Tshivenda
Language of mass media alone	Chichewa
No role	Baswa, Hwesa, Kunda, Nambya, Chisena, Sesotho, Tshwa, IsiXhosa

Source: Based on Hachipola (1996)

rather be considered as resources for people's aspirations and full participation in national development.

Abuse of African Languages as a National Resource

All resources, whether physical or human, are only valuable if society
recognises their value, manages them properly and puts them to the right
use. Thus, gold and diamonds are regarded as valuable commodities
because society has attached to them both economic and social value.
Although gold and diamonds bring wealth to nations, they have also
caused disaster and misery in countries such as Angola, Liberia and Sierra
Leone. Similarly, wildlife can be beneficial to a country as it attracts
tourism and trade, hence contributing to the economy, or it can be a source
of food for the people. But again, where it has been mismanaged, it has
depleted rapidly, causing environmental instability and resulting, therefore, in disaster for humans. Equally, although people can provide the
much-needed labour in a nation's development, any misuse of such human
resources, such as underpayment or forced labour, may lead to strikes,
riots or national strife.

Language, like all other societal resources, needs to be properly managed
and used. The abuse or mismanagement of a language can result in problems, which may involve individuals, groups of people or the whole nation.
We will now review some of the problems, common in Africa, whose origins
lie in the abuse of languages as a national resource.

While African languages can be used to enhance solidarity among the speakers, there are times when they have also been used as divisive tools. Since, as we saw above, a common language is the most conspicuous feature in group identity, it can be used to divide people according to ethnicity, causing hostilities, particularly in countries where ethnic conflicts are already in existence. This was, and in some cases still is, the situation in such countries as Angola, the Democratic Republic of Congo, Sierra Leone and Liberia, to mention but a few. Of course, language is not the only basis of identity, as in countries like Burundi, Rwanda and Somalia belligerent groups have identified themselves by other features.

Since language may be considered a means by which participation is facilitated or prevented, it holds the key to the establishment of a true democracy and equality in a country (Bamgbose, 2000). In most African countries, speakers of minority languages are excluded from or marginalised in respect of national participation because of the use, by the ruling elite, of an ex-colonial language or of a dominant indigenous language, which may be used as a lingua franca but not understood by certain groups. Speakers of minority languages are thereby denied direct participation in public interaction, meaningful audiences with government authorities, contact with other groups or active contribution at public rallies. The exclusion of minority language speakers for these reasons is very common in Africa, as most countries either assume that all are able to follow discourse in those languages or insist that all official communication be made in them whatever the social cost. But, as has been shown (Bamgbose, 2000: 15), the minority languages taken together account for a substantial proportion of the population in a country. In Ghana, for example, minority language speakers constitute 44% of the population, while in Nigeria they make up at least 36% of the population. It is therefore unfortunate that many African heads of state deliver key national speeches – which touch on most people's lives – in English, French or Portuguese solely because one of these happens to be the official language even if the majority of their people do not understand a word or understand only partially.

A language can be used as a barrier to social advancement. The lack of knowledge of a language or non-possession of the required proficiency in the high-level ex-colonial language (as official language) or in the nationally dominant language (as lingua franca or national language) may prevent or impede social mobility. Following Heine (1970), African languages can be categorised as those which, in their social roles, are horizontal and those which are vertical. Whereas the horizontal languages stress solidarity and social equality, as is characteristic of mother tongues, the vertical languages stress divergence and inequality – particularly separation from the masses

– and thereby serve as a means for upward social mobility. This is characteristic of the ex-colonial languages. Hence, the motivation for speaking English, French or Portuguese is not so much the need to communicate in an international language but is mainly the desire to break barriers and be able to move up the social scale.

As we have seen, many language policies in African states have tended to ignore the minority languages. In most cases these languages have been accorded no public function or specific use. This has caused their speakers to devalue them, or to develop negative attitudes towards them, as not useful in their socio-economic activities. Such negative attitudes lead them either to abandon their mother tongue or to depend on the majority languages, in which their proficiency may not be as good as that of the mother-tongue speakers.

Last, as we mentioned above, languages are often used as tools of socialisation and solidarity between the speakers. However, such use may sometimes be in conflict with modes of politeness. It is expected that when a third party is present who does not understand the language that two interlocutors are using, another more common language (usually a lingua franca or ex-colonial language) should be used. Although this is the norm in most situations, there are cases where people ignore others in their conversation or speeches, either deliberately or through lack of awareness. When this is done deliberately in a situation where the third party could expect to be part of the discussion or where polite modes call for the use of a common language, there is a clear case of abuse of the principles of politeness and social understanding. In Africa, such abuse normally occurs where speakers of major languages are putting pressure on those of lesser languages to be part of the major language sphere of influence or where the elite want to distinguish themselves from the masses through the use of an ex-colonial language.

Summary and Conclusions

Although communication is the most important function of language in human life, languages fulfill other functions, which include cultural transmission, self-identity, socialisation, group solidarity, marking of social relations and reflection of social stratification. Hence, language is central in our lives as it is not only essential in our social interactions and relations, but also important in distinguishing us and ascertaining our positions in society. The social significance of language is even more important in Africa, where interactive activities and relational hierarchies in family and village life are well entrenched in societal traditions and practices.

Moreover, African languages constitute a source of considerable value for humanity in general, and for the countries where they are spoken in particular. This is because languages can be regarded as resources, just like minerals and wildlife. Their value is to be found in their linguistic, cultural and artistic attributes. African languages have, in many cases, linguistic features that are rare or even unique among the languages of the world. Such phenomena are important not only in understanding the nature of human language, but also in contributing to our knowledge of the possible variations in human languages. Moreover, African languages display an extensive cultural wealth that has been accumulated over the centuries of each language's existence. Each reflects a unique world vision formed by its speakers through their long experience of their environment. At the same time, most African languages manifest a rich range of artistic phenomena. One unique practice in many African societies is the joking relationship between ethnic groups or certain members of the family.

From another perspective, African languages, if used to their full potential, could be vehicles of national development, as they would ensure the positive and active participation of all the people in a country. Unfortunately, many African governments have taken a short-cut by adopting an ex-colonial language to the exclusion of others on the pretext that they are already technically developed to deal with formal and scientific discourse or because they are considered to be ethnically neutral.

Although they are important linguistic, cultural and artistic resources and, potentially, vehicles for development, languages can be abused. The abuse includes their use for divisive purposes between groups, to exclude others from participation in national affairs, to impede the social advancement of certain sectors of the population, to marginalise the speakers of other languages and to deliberately exclude others from participating in discussions with others.

Thus, language is an important resource in human life and can be a source of great value for a nation as well as being part of national heritage. However, most African countries have either not paid enough attention to the language issue or have adopted the attitude of 'let sleeping dogs lie', and, thus, have made little effort to ensure the optimal use of the linguistic resources with which they are endowed. In many cases, these resources have been abused, with the consequence that the masses, who usually form the majority in a country, are excluded from national affairs because of the use of an ex-colonial language in official matters; or, similarly, the speakers of minority languages, who may form a sizable proportion of the country's population, are excluded from national affairs because of the use of a dominant language. Usually it is the speakers of the minority languages who suffer the most as they receive a double blow. As a result, they tend to learn and use the dominant language as a second language or even shift to it at the expense of their mother tongue. This is because they find the dominant language both socially and economically more attractive. Hence, the fate of the minority languages is clear: that of doom and extinction.

Chapter 4

The Minority Languages of Africa

The Position of the Minority Languages

From the foregoing chapters it is clear that, although Africa is a pluri-lingual and multicultural continent, there is no equity in the status or roles accorded to the various languages spoken in the more than 50 nation-states and territories of Africa. Most states have preferred to accord the prestigious national roles to an ex-colonial language and/or to the nationally or major dominant languages. In most cases, the minority languages have been either neglected or marginalised to the extent of not being assigned any public function. Hence they remain largely family, intra-ethnic or cultural media. In some cases they have been given symbolic status as national languages, or even official languages, but with no socio-economic or public function attached to them. In most cases, the neglected or marginalised languages are also demographically inferior, hence their designation as minority languages. This term is also extensively used in the social sciences (Mazonde, 2002). In this section, we shall discuss the status, role and future of the minority languages of Africa.

Sociolinguistically, a minority language is defined not only by its relative demographic inferiority but also, and more so, by its limited public functions (Batibo 2001a: 124). Thus, a minority language can be identified horizontally by looking at its weak or non-dominant position in relation to other languages in the region or nation, and vertically on the basis of its low status and absence of use in public or official areas. Following this definition, most of the African languages would be designated as minority languages in view of their relative demographic, political and socio-economic inferiority. Most are confined to family and village communication.

In fact, it is their marginalisation and exclusion from serving in *secondary domains* (that is, public functions) as well as having no social status or prestige, that most characterises them as minority languages. It is for this reason that the ex-colonial languages, although spoken by just a few educated people in most countries, are not considered to be minority languages. For example, English is not considered a minority language in Namibia

Table 9 Status of the languages in Botswana

Status	Language	Number
Ex-colonial language (official language)	English	1
Nationally dominant language (national language)	Setswana	1
Areally dominant languages	Ikalanga, Shekgalagari, Naro	3
Minority languages	Thimbukushu, Otjiherero, Nama, ǂHua, Zezuru, Nambya, Sindebele, Sebirwa, Shiyeyi, Afrikaans, Chikuhane, Tshwa, Setswapong, Silozi, !Xóõ, Shua, Kwedam, Ju|'hoan, Kua, |Gwi, Rugciriku, ǂKx'au||'ein, ||Gana	23

although it is spoken by only 3% of the population. On the other hand, a language like Rukwangali, which is spoken by a much larger percentage of the Namibian population, is regarded as a minority language because of its lack of socio-economic prestige and public function, inferior social status, and not having any national or areal impact. The only non-minority languages are, according to our definition, the ex-colonial and the (nationally or areally) dominant languages.

As described in Chapter 2, the language situation in most African countries is typified by the presence of three types of language – an ex-colonial language; one or several dominant languages at national and areal levels; and minority languages. In most countries the minority languages are in the majority by far. Botswana provides a good example. As shown in Table 9, of the 28 languages spoken in the country, 23 are minority languages, while three are areally dominant and one is nationally dominant.

From Table 9 it is clear that the majority of the languages of Botswana are minority languages. However, although they constitute 82% of the number of languages in the country, their speakers make up only about 7% of the population. Some of them, such as ǂHua, \|Gwi and \|\|Gana, are spoken by scarcely 1000 people. On the other hand, although Ikalanga, Shekgalagari and Naro are areally important, they have no tangible public function. It is because of their dynamism and socio-historical circumstances that they have assumed areal importance.

Table 10 Proportions of minority languages in the African countries

	Minority languages as percentage of total	Countries or territories
1	0–19	Burundi, Canary Islands, Cape Verde, Djibouti, Lesotho, Mayotte, Reunion, Rwanda, Seychelles, Swaziland
2	20–39	Comoro Islands, Egypt, Eritrea, Mauritania, Mauritius, Niger, São Tomé e Principe
3	40–59	Gambia, Guinea, Guinea-Bissau, Libya, Madagascar, Malawi, Mali, Morocco, Sierra Leone, South Africa, Tunisia, Uganda, Zambia, Zimbabwe
4	60–79	Algeria, Angola, Burkina Faso, Central African Republic, Côte d'Ivoire, Equatorial Guinea, Ghana, Kenya, Liberia, Mozambique, Namibia, Senegal, Somalia, Sudan, Togo
5	>80	Botswana, Cameroon, Chad, Congo Republic, Democratic Republic of Congo, Ethiopia, Gabon, Nigeria, Tanzania

Looking at the continent as a whole, the countries of Africa could be categorised according to the percentage of the minority languages in relation to the total number of languages spoken in a country. According to our survey, the scenario would be as set out in Table 10.

Obviously, the above repartition is highly arbitrary as it is based on our classification of the nationally and areally dominant languages as opposed to the minority languages. As one may notice, the highest proportions of the minority languages are found in countries either with a large number of languages, such as Nigeria, Cameroon, the Democratic Republic of Congo, Chad and Tanzania, or where there is a marked imbalance between the dominant language(s) and the minority languages, as in the case of Botswana and Gabon. It is in the category where the percentage of minority languages is highest that language domination is most critical. As shown in Appendix 3, of a total of 2477 languages spoken in the various African countries, 1931 are minority languages. This means that such languages, in spite of their relatively few speakers, constitute 78.0% of the African languages. One should note, however, that the total of 2477 languages given in Appendix 3 is misleading as a number are spoken in several countries and hence have been counted several times. For example, Kiswahili has been counted 11 times as it is spoken in Tanzania, Kenya, Uganda, Burundi, Rwanda, Somalia, the Democratic Republic of Congo, Zambia, Malawi, Mozambique and Comoro. If we count each language in the continent only once, the total of languages in Africa according to our figures would be 2193. As a proportion of this figure, the percentage of the minority languages is 81.9%

Common Characteristics of the Minority Languages

Although the most basic and conspicuous features of minority languages are their small number of speakers, low status and absence of public functions, they are also characterised by other features. The minority languages are usually not sufficiently described. As a result, most do not have standardised orthographies or appropriate grammars and dictionaries. The absence of documentation is often one of the excuses advanced by decision-makers against their use in education or other public functions.

Such languages are usually limited to cultural use in the villages where they are spoken. They are not technicised enough to handle technical fields or Western concepts. Again, this is one of the excuses used to discourage the adoption of these languages in education or other public functions. There is often a historical legacy of domination by the dominant languages. Such historical experiences tend to make the speakers feel inferior to those who speak the widely used languages. They often lack self-esteem and readily abandon their language, culture and even self-identity in favour of the more widely used languages. The language and culture often become a stigma. Thus, in many parts of Africa, speakers of the less widely used languages readily adopt personal names from the larger languages, such as Arabic, Hausa, Kiswahili or Setswana, where these are spoken.

Minority language speakers tend to develop negative attitudes towards their mother tongue, not only because of the often painful historical legacies but also because of the lack of socio-economic opportunities its use is perceived to offer, and they may consider it advantageous to adopt the more widely used language for their children's education, job-seeking and wider communication. As we have seen, the speakers of many minority languages often encourage their children to learn the more widely used languages to enhance their future opportunities and skills. So the number of those who speak minority languages as their mother tongue diminishes from generation to generation. This in turn gives rise to language shift and death. Under such circumstances, the future of the minority languages in Africa is bleak.

Disadvantages Suffered by Minority Language Speakers

The speakers of minority languages usually become victims of a number of disadvantages in society due to their linguistic and cultural background. Most of these disadvantages are social or cultural, but they may also affect their educational and economic well-being.

Speakers of minority languages often find themselves in a dilemma as, on the one hand, they wish to maintain their linguistic, cultural and ethnic identity so as to preserve their origins and self-identity, but, on the other hand, they would like to integrate in the wider community so as to have access to education, paid jobs and interaction with the wider world via a widely used language and culture. Opting for the first means marginalisation, and opting for the second leads to loss of identity.

Minority languages often suffer from historical legacies of domination by the larger or more widely used languages. Hence the speakers tend to have a low estimation of their languages and culture. This is particularly true of the Khoesan languages of southern Africa, which have suffered long years at the hands of mainly Bantu speakers (Batibo, 1998; Crawhall, 1998). Many children of the minority language speakers, who have been brought up in a particular cultural and socio-economic setting, find it difficult to adjust to the new social environment when they start school. They are often torn between two worlds, as described by Ngugi wa Thiong'o (1965). The problem is even more acute where children are based in rural or remote areas. The findings of Le Roux (1999), for example, show that most Khoesan-speaking children in southern Africa are torn between their own nature-based environment and the radically different environment of the majority language or Western-based school. As a result, many Khoesan children run away from school for reasons not only of environmental incompatibility, but also, and mainly, linguistic and cultural differences (Batibo, 2001a). Such findings are similar to the observations of Selolwane (1995), who discovered that the high drop-out rate among Khoesan school children was brought about by the alien nature of the school environment itself, including linguistic and cultural differences. Cases like this are widespread in other parts of Africa, as reported in studies by Acquaye (1968), Erny (1973), Laye (1966) and Ohuche & Otaala (1981). All these studies describe the incompatible relationship between the child's home environment and that of the school.

The minority language-speaking children who start school are often at a gross disadvantage as the language of the primary school is generally the chosen national medium or the ex-colonial language. Unless the chosen national medium and environment are close to the children's background, their learning process will be substantially hampered as they will not have mastered their mother tongues fully by the time the new medium of instruction is encountered. This prevents the child from transferring prior knowledge to the new environment. Furthermore, an inadequate mastery of the medium of instruction will not facilitate proper cognitive and affective development in these young learners (Batibo, 2001a: 126). This builds a false foundation for the children (Sure, 2000; UNESCO, 1953). It has been observed that European children are faster and more assertive in learning, while African children are slower and lack confidence. If this observation is true, the answer is not in the race or culture of the African children but rather in their linguistic and environmental attributes, as most of them do not start school in their home languages or in familiar environments. Most African children learn through media and environments that do not reflect experience in their home communities. They grapple simultaneously with an insufficiently known language and alien environment. One important aspect of confidence and assertiveness is mastery of a language.

It has been demonstrated in four separate studies carried out by the Association of the Development of Education in Africa (ADEA) in various African countries in the past three decades – namely Nigeria (1970), Tanzania (1971), Mali (1985) and South Africa (1990) – that children learn faster and performed better if taught in their mother tongue rather than in another language (ADEA Working Group 1996a: 5). The ADEA Working Group (*ibid.*: 6) also established that there is a close relationship between language proficiency, thought and intelligence. Thus, without good language support neither thought nor intelligence can be properly developed in a young learner. In countries where a national language is used as a medium of instruction at primary school level, such as Akan in Ghana, Yoruba in Nigeria or Setswana in Botswana, it was thought that the use of an indigenous medium would facilitate learning for all children. But studies have shown that even in such cases the minority language speakers – who have limited proficiency in the educational medium when they start school – are strongly disadvantaged, and that many of them drop out early from school for that reason (Legère, 1992; Selolwane, 1995).

As pointed out in Chapter 3, language may be considered as a means by which participation is facilitated or prevented. With their limited knowledge of the official and/or national languages, minority language speakers may find it difficult to participate in public forums, deal with local administrators or government authorities, attend properly to financial transactions that concern them or make contact with other groups. In addition, they are often denied knowledge of what is going on around them because they do not know the official or dominant language used in the mass media. According to a study carried out by Batibo & Mosaka (2000), many of the speakers of the minority languages in Botswana, for example, have no access to information provided in the form of radio announcements, newspaper publications and public rallies, where the information is conveyed in English or Setswana. Hence, inhabitants of many remote villages have little or no information about topical issues such as the HIV/AIDS pandemic, the outbreak of other dangerous diseases, modern farming methods to increase crop yields, sudden increases in the crime rate and the like. Thus the non-use of minority languages in public life has not only marginalised or excluded their speakers but has also rendered them less confident and less assertive in their approach to public issues. This has, in turn, led to them being unable to contribute fully to national development.

Finally, the speakers of minority languages are often disadvantaged socio-economically because in the world of commerce and commodity exchange the dominant languages are normally used as trade languages. Those who speak them fluently, whether as a first or second language, usually make better deals, convince buyers and are able to interact easily. In contrast, most minority language speakers are at a disadvantage in this area of activity. Moreover, in some countries such as Kenya, fluency in the national language, Kiswahili, is essential in obtaining certain jobs, just as English is necessary for high-level jobs. Most of those with limited proficiency are the up-country minority language speakers. These are therefore often denied job opportunities because of their linguistic background.

From the above, it is clear that minority language speakers are in a disadvantaged position culturally, politically, socio-economically and educationally because of their linguistic background. They are easily marginalised in public life or denied essential services because they lack the means to gain the attention of the relevant authority.

Some Misgivings About the Minority Languages

While minority language speakers are often disadvantaged because of their linguistic background, the problem is compounded by misgivings by both scholars and governments about their value to a country, particularly in national development. In many African countries, minority languages have been regarded as a problem or a negative factor in development. This outlook has recently been supported by some scholars, such as Robinson (1996) and Watson (1994), who argue that although no causal relationship has been established between linguistic diversity and economic development, it has been observed that the highest concentrations of language diversity are found in the less economically developed countries. In other words, the poorest groups of countries in the world, including those of Africa, are found in those areas which are the most plurilingual. One may dismiss this observation as a mere coincidence, and we wish to assert that plurilingualism in itself is not a cause of underdevelopment, but that it all depends on what people do with it. They may use it as a divisive means so that attention is focused on conflict rather than development. Or they may use plurilingualism to disadvantage minority language speakers so that their mental capabilities are inadequately developed and they are left behind in developmental efforts. In Africa the children of minority language speakers have to use another language in their early years in the school system. As a result, they are unable to develop proper cognitive, in-depth and creatively independent skills and techniques. In most Third World countries the languages used in the educational system and vocational training are not those that the children have grown up speaking in their respective homes. This certainly affects their performance not only at school but also later in their adult or professional life.

Even if there is a will to accommodate the minority languages in a country's language policy and to use them in national development, many African countries find it impractical to develop and use all the languages spoken within their borders as it would be too costly. Certainly, it would be a costly option if a country were to develop and use all or most of the languages for all public functions, as South Africa has endeavoured to do. This is costly not only in terms of developing all the languages but also in providing expertise in areas such as translation and interpretation. In the process, much time would also be wasted. Here it is important to use the principle of rationalisation, whereby a nation makes an optimal selection, development and use of its languages at a cost it can afford, as we noted has been done in Zimbabwe in Chapter 3. Where possible a cluster of related languages could be codified, standardised or used together, as has been successfully done in Uganda, where only six clusters were identified out of the 33 languages (Ladefoged *et al.*, 1972). Evidently, the use of a minority language in the public sphere would depend on how many speak the language, the level of standardisation and documentation of the language, speakers' attitudes, levels of vitality, the degree of sustenance such a policy would require and resource availability.

One other misgiving about the promotion and use of the indigenous languages is that such a move breeds tribalism and ethnicity, which are fearful ills in most African countries. Again, the Ugandan experience has shown that people become more nationalistic and co-operative in national affairs once they realise that their language and culture are being accorded respect. This is also true of a country like Malawi, where the former President Kamuzu Banda imposed Chichewa as the sole national language, much to the disapproval of most other groups. However, when the new government of President Bakili Muluzi put the other languages on the same footing as Chichewa, the co-operation of the other groups in national affairs was regained. The problems of ethnicity and tribalism are not bred by language or culture, but rather by those who wish to use these attributes for divisive or personal ends. The answer to ethnic conflicts is not to suppress plurilingual and multicultural diversity but to recognise it and allow it to flourish in an atmosphere of equality and understanding.

Given that the present trend is towards a global village, a world of information technology and a sophisticated lifestyle, English is in the lead as the super-international language, followed by other world languages such as French and Spanish. In view of this trend the minority languages, which are usually associated with a set of traditional practices, beliefs and knowledge, are seen in the eyes of the 'modernists' as backward and out of tune with the present. Such people would not mind seeing these languages die in the name of modernity and globalisation. In some African countries the tendency to neglect the minority languages has been driven by the desire to promote a strong national language. Tanzania, which was determined to use Kiswahili as the sole national language, reached a point where there was no concern at a governmental level if the other languages disappeared in the process. Thus, its former President, Julius Nyerere, addressing the Tanzania Kiswahili Writers Association in 1984, admitted that the high-level empowerment of Kiswahili as the national language was likely to affect the other languages in the country. To him this was an inevitable development, inasmuch as good moves often have side effects that are likely to be adverse (Batibo, 1992: 93). The crucial question here is whether we should allow the loss of linguistic diversity in the African countries for the sake of a single national language that is often equated with unity and identity.

Also, in some African countries there are other forces that tend to undermine the use of minority languages. One of these forces is religion. Some religions, particularly Islam, tend to associate certain languages with the faith and even to make these languages a part of the lives of the faithful. Arabic is the language that is generally associated with Islam all over the world. But Kiswahili, which was for a long time associated with the Arab traders along the eastern coast, has also come to be regarded as the language of Islam, and many converts to Islam resort to it as their primary language. This has caused many speakers of minority languages to abandon their languages in favour of Kiswahili. The same has been reported of

Hausa and Fulfude in West Africa, which are also associated with Islam, particularly in northern Nigeria, Niger and Burkina Faso. Hence many converts tend to shift to them on religious grounds.

Finally, even where minority languages are still vibrant, there is a progressive limitation in the acquisition of knowledge, along with the relevant vocabulary, of indigenous phenomena by the younger generation. This is happening not only because most children spend much of their time in school rather than in their home environment, but also because there has been a dramatic destruction of fauna and flora in most of the African countries as well as an abandonment of many of the traditional customs and cultural practices. Most parents are aware of this trend but, seeing themselves incapable of reversing it, reluctantly allow it in the name of the 'modern advancement' of their children.

Summary and Conclusions

Due to the lack of equity in the status and functions of the languages of Africa, some find themselves in a disadvantaged position. These are the minority languages, which are usually not only demographically inferior but are also marginalised in that they do not have any tangible public function. In fact, most of the African languages are minority languages. These languages are often characterised by insufficient codification, limited domains of use, legacies of domination by other languages, negative attitudes towards them by their speakers and active bilingualism in the more publicly used languages.

As a result, speakers of minority languages tend to suffer a number of disadvantages, which include being in a dilemma over the choice between expressing self-identity through the use of their mother tongue or integration into the larger community by shifting to the dominant language. Moreover, the speakers of minority languages experience many other disadvantages, such as the low esteem in which their languages are held, the problems their children experience in the unfamiliar linguistic environment of school, marginalisation or exclusion from participation in national affairs because they are unable to speak the dominant language, or finding they are hampered in their socio-economic dealings for the same reasons. At another level, there have been misgivings about the utility or even developmental value of the minority languages, particularly as they tend to be found in economically backward countries, where they are often associated with underdevelopment, tribalism and ethnicity.

The foregoing is a clear indication that there are many forces in Africa emanating from both within and without that make it difficult to promote the minority languages or accord them viable public functions. In the eyes of many they are a liability rather than an asset in African developmental endeavours. It is not surprising, therefore, that the language policies of very few African countries make explicit reference to them in relation to national development. Most policies either ignore them completely, as in Botswana, or accord them mere symbolic status as national languages, as in Namibia, with no active role. As a result, most of these languages have become highly vulnerable as their speakers do not see any tangible value in them and would therefore be prepared to abandon them in favour of languages that offer greater socio-economic benefits. Many parents are happy to see their children become proficient in languages that give them access to education, job opportunities and a better standard of living.

Chapter 5

The Endangered Languages of Africa

Definition of an Endangered Language

The term *endangered language* has become common in current socio-linguistic literature, just like the terms *language shift* and *language death*. In the current use of the term it denotes a language that is threatened by extinction. The threat may come because the pool of speakers is declining rapidly to small numbers, because the younger generations are not learning to speak it, or because the domains in which the language is used have shrunk so much that it is not used regularly in the language community. The other situation would be that the linguistic structures of a language are so eroded and simplified that the language is progressively becoming non-functional. The first set of situations could be considered as sociolinguistic as they describe how a language is used in society, while the last would fall under structural linguistics as this looks at the structure of a language and its functional capability. Usually, the two sets of situations occur simultaneously as a language that is not being used frequently in the various domains will start to shrink. As a consequence, its stylistic and structural variations and complexities gradually become eroded or simplified to a non-functional level.

Another perspective on an endangered language is given by Bobaljik *et al.* (1996), who regard it as one that will have no speakers left within a few generations. Clearly, it would be unrealistic and simplistic to consider the existence of a dichotomy between 'endangered' and 'non-endangered' languages. It is more accurate to regard language endangerment as a continuum, or a sliding scale, with 'safe' languages at one end and 'dying' languages at the other. If we were to place the African languages on such a scale, we would identify some of them as relatively 'safe', while the others would be placed on the 'highly endangered' part of the scale. In general, the minority languages would be the ones which would be found in the 'endangered' zone, as many of them would manifest the main features of endangered languages.

On the other hand, if we go by the predictions of Michael Krauss of the Alaska Native Language Centre (Krauss, 1992: 7), by the beginning of the next century the world will see 'the death or doom of 90% of mankind's languages'. According to these predictions, therefore, by the year 2100 the world will have only about 650 of the present 6528 languages (see Grimes, 2000). Since Africa harbours over 30% of the world's languages, only about 200 languages would remain there, less than 10% of the present number. Although this may appear to be an extreme or exaggerated scenario, it nevertheless points up the gravity of the problem as the pressure on African languages comes not only from within but also from many and complex forces at work in the wider world.

Factors Likely to Cause Language Endangerment

In normal circumstances, no community would like to see its language die as a language provides a communicative and interactive lifeline for its speakers. Also in a normal situation, no community would be prepared to abandon its language in favour of another since, as we saw above, one's language is not only a tool for communication and a vehicle of cultural accumulation and transmission but is also the symbol of one's identity and self-expression. Any speaker of a language that is in a weak position will struggle to resist pressure from a stronger language. The degree of success in resisting the stronger language will depend on three factors: the degree of pressure exerted by that language; the amount of resistance put up by speakers of the weaker language; and the relative gains if those speakers were to yield to the pressure to give way. Any process of language shift results from either weak resistance to the stronger language or the voluntary abandonment of a language by its speakers on account of specific socio-economic gains conferred by the majority language. Thus, we have three possible scenarios.

- If the degree of pressure from the stronger language is greater than the resistance offered, the weaker language is highly endangered. The pressure from the stronger language group could take the form of political domination, socio-economic attraction or social gains. One example is that of the nomadic Masaai in East Africa, who are known to dominate the smaller language groups, forcing them to abandon their languages in favour of Maasai (Brenzinger, 1992; Dimmendaal, 1992).
- If the amount of resistance by the weaker language is greater than the pressure from the stronger language, the weaker language is not in danger. The high degree of resistance could be due to strong

traditional or religious attachment, as in the case of Coptic in Egypt, or a strong sense of self-assertion and determination, as in the case of the Kiswahili-Makonde speakers in Durban, who have managed to resist language shift in spite of their small number.

- If the weaker language speakers see many advantages in joining the community of the stronger language speakers, they may not resist at all but abandon their language in favour of the other as a strategy for integration. This was the case of the immigrant communities in Austria, as reported by Gal (1979).

When two languages of unequal socio-political or economic strength come into contact, a pressure–resistance relationship will arise (Figure 3). Language endangerment becomes apparent when there is a net loss of resistance on the part of the weaker language. As the weaker language is overpowered, the first indicators of endangerment and the beginning of the process towards extinction start to appear. These first indicators involve a highly bilingual situation in which the weaker language community speaks both its mother tongue and the stronger language. At first the stronger language is used mainly in secondary domains, particularly in inter-ethnic communication. Gradually, however, its use may expand into some of the primary domains where the weaker language was originally the means of communication. At the same time there is a growing parental indifference to how well children learn the mother tongue, inasmuch as they are no longer strict about how perfectly it is acquired or if it is acquired at all. The children learn the mother tongue less and less perfectly and may learn only fragments of it, giving more attention to the stronger language, which becomes increasingly dominant in their lives. As a result, the weaker language is used less frequently and its stylistic and structural complexities may start to erode or simplify. This scenario is schematised in Table 11.

As shown in Table 11, there are several indicators of an endangered language, which may be divided into three categories. The first category is attitude-related in that the speakers of a language develop a negative attitude to it and therefore become ambivalent in their loyalty and indifferent about teaching the language to their children. The second category of indicators is language use-related in that not only does transmission of the

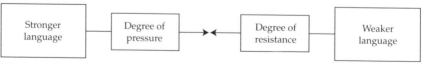

Figure 3 Pressure and resistance in language endangerment

Table 11 Common indicators of an endangered language

Indicator type	Common indicators
Attitude-related	• Development of negative attitudes towards own language • Ambivalent language loyalty • Indifference about language transfer to children • Association of mother tongue with low economic and social status
Language-use related	• Inactive transmission of language to children • Reduction in domains of use • Diminishing number of speakers
Language-structure related	• Limited stylistic variation • Structural erosion and simplification • Lexical reduction

language become inactive but also the language is used in very few, mainly primary, domains. Moreover, the number of speakers diminishes progressively as they shift to the dominant language. Finally, the third category is language structure-related in that the language becomes considerably limited in its stylistic variation and the structure is drastically eroded or simplified. At the same time there is substantial lexical reduction, so that the language can no longer be used effectively in any discourse.

It must be stated here that these indicators do not all appear at the same time, nor do they appear with the same intensity. Usually, the attitude-related indicators appear, and very visibly, before those related to language use. The structure-related indicators tend to appear as the terminal stage of language extinction looms.

It is important, too, to stress that a limited number of speakers or the seemingly moribund state of a language is not a prerequisite, but rather a favourable condition, for language endangerment. As demonstrated by Batibo (1992), even language communities with more than 200,000 ethnic members, such as those traditionally speaking Kizaramo and Kibondei, both in Tanzania, are highly threatened in view of their location in the heart of the Kiswahili zone. Similar remarks were made by Krauss (1992) about Breton, with a membership of over 1 million people, but fast giving way to French despite many modern approaches to its preservation. It is the decline in the transmission process of a language that is cause for the greatest alarm.

A Survey of the Endangered Languages of Africa
General observations

In carrying out any survey of the endangered languages, one crucial question to consider first is: at what stage of endangerment should a language be regarded as actually endangered? This is because we are dealing with a continuum ranging from 'relatively safe' to 'nearly extinct'. There are, therefore, many interpretations of language endangerment, just as one would expect if a survey were to be conducted in hospitals on death-threatened patients. One extreme would be to take all people with serious infections or conditions, such as HIV, SARS, cancer, heart problems, kidney failure, liver ailments and the like; while another extreme would be to record only the cases of patients in a critical condition. Evidently, the results would not be the same. The same obtains when sociolinguists and ethnographers attempt to document the endangered languages. Moreover, information on many of the languages is either scanty, totally unavailable or contradictory. Hence, many of the conclusions are highly speculative.

There have been several attempts to document the endangered and, in some instances, the already extinct languages of Africa. These attempts have ranged from a consideration of the whole of Africa through regional, national, and individual cases. As pointed out above, the criteria have differed from one researcher to another. So the numbers obtained have also differed.

One of the most important sets of studies was begun nearly 50 years ago by the Summer Institute of Linguistics (SIL) based in Dallas, USA. These surveys are meant to document the sociolinguistic status of the world's languages, including the state of the languages. A number of publications in different editions have resulted and have been issued under the name of *Ethnologue*, currently edited by Barbara Grimes. Although the information is primarily meant to assist organisations translating the Bible throughout the world, it is also relevant and useful in scholarly circles. The other survey that has covered the whole of Africa is one by Gabriele Sommer, who recorded more than 150 extinct or nearly extinct languages in Africa (Sommer, 1992). Most of her sources were secondary and therefore diverse in quality, reliability and coverage. The study nonetheless provided important information on each of the languages involved. The third continent-wide survey of the endangered languages is one currently being undertaken at SOAS, London, by the Endangered Languages Documentation Programme. This survey is also basically documentary, relying heavily on already existing sources, such as *Ethnologue* and a number of others. The Programme has so far managed to list a significant number of languages that are presumed to be extinct or nearly extinct on the African continent and in other parts of the world. These languages are listed by country.

As expected, most are from countries where there are large numbers of languages, such as Nigeria, Cameroon, Chad, Ethiopia and Sudan. One other general source is the survey of minority languages of the world by Harald Haarmann (2001), which lists some of the most threatened languages of the world, including those of Africa.

Two important volumes, both edited by Matthias Brenzinger, contain important regional, national and individual surveys of endangered and extinct languages (Brenzinger 1992, 1998). They include Hayward's study of the endangered languages of Ethiopia, in which he identifies three highly threatened languages that have unique morphological features of theoretical interest (Hayward, 1998); Blench's survey of the status of the languages of central Nigeria, in which he demonstrates that of the 395 languages spoken in the Middle Belt, 96 had only 400 speakers or fewer, 24 were highly threatened, 11 were presumed extinct and some were developing into complex cases of pidginisation (Blench, 1998); Connell's study of the moribund languages of the linguistically most concentrated region in the world, the Nigeria–Cameroon borderland, where at least 50 languages had less than 1000 speakers and were therefore highly threatened, while 18 languages were presumed to be in a dying state (Connell, 1998). Moreover, Kiyoshi Shimizu had earlier carried out a survey of the southern Bauchi group of Chadic languages, which found more than 80% of the 62 languages covered to be vanishing (Shimizu, 1978). There are also two separate studies by the present author and Karsten Legère, respectively, on the state of the languages of Tanzania, in which they show that, due to the predominance of Kiswahili and other areally dominant languages, most of the small languages among the more than 120 ethnic languages in the country are highly threatened, while at least five are presumed extinct (Batibo, 1992; Legère, 1992). My own studies of the endangered languages of Botswana single out 12 of the 28 languages spoken in the country as highly threatened. Many of these highly endangered languages are of Khoesan origin (Batibo, 1997, 1998). These studies were followed by a volume edited by myself and Birgit Smieja in which more details of the threatened minority languages were presented (Batibo & Smieja, 2000). Traill (1995) carried out a survey of the extinct or nearly extinct Khoesan languages of southern Africa in which he showed that at least seven languages have disappeared in the last few centuries. Finally, two major studies have been undertaken recently that include catalogues of the endangered world languages; these are the *Atlas of the World's Languages in Danger of Disappearing* by Stephen A. Wurm (1996) and the UNESCO website, based in Tokyo, Japan, for which Bernd Heine and Matthias Brezinger have provided the data on Africa (UNESCO 2003a).

Apart from the above studies, there are other surveys that have been carried out mainly on individual languages. The number of such studies has been growing rapidly as more and more scholars have become aware of the bleak future of many of Africa's minority languages.

There appear to be regional imbalances in the distribution of studies on the endangered languages. While research has concentrated on regions such as eastern Africa, southern Africa and the Nigeria–Cameroon region, only scant research has been conducted on the endangered languages of central and northern Africa or the Atlantic parts of West Africa. It is quite noticeable that the thrust of research on endangered languages has tended to be in the English-speaking regions. This is not surprising as sociolinguistic studies have been more actively pursued in the English-speaking world than in the French-speaking world. The latter has remained primarily descriptively orientated, as manifested by many of the productions of French research centres, such as LACITO (*Langues et Civilisations à Tradition Orale*) and LLACAN (*Langage, Langues et Cultures d'Afrique Noire*) in Paris. Of course, such descriptive research is vital in the documentation process of the endangered languages. A number of German organisations such as the German Research Foundation and the Volkswagen Foundation have been very supportive of studies and symposia on endangered languages. As a result, substantial German-based research and documentation has been undertaken on a number of cases of endangered languages in Africa.

It is now becoming common at international linguistics conferences for there to be a substantial number of presentations on endangered languages. This has enabled such fora to discuss and even raise concern on the endangered languages as well as providing for the publication of research findings in conference proceedings. Many of the case studies on endangered languages have included a description of some of the unique features of the relevant languages that are of theoretical or comparative value in linguistics studies. Such studies have been of remarkable utility. Moreover, it is gratifying to note from the increasing number of studies on the endangered languages that both foreign and local scholars are becoming involved in research in this area.

Country-by-country case studies

In this section we shall present an overview of the endangered and extinct or nearly extinct languages in each African country. We shall also highlight the country's language situation in terms of the country's overall population, the number of languages and the pattern of language dominance. Then, for each country a list of the highly endangered and extinct or nearly extinct languages will be given.

The languages that are described as highly endangered are those which are currently deemed to be most vulnerable on the basis of a set of indicators which were used in the survey. These indicators included:

- The number of speakers currently using the language. In this survey, all minority languages spoken by fewer than 5000 people were considered to be endangered, particularly if other factors were involved.
- The degree of bilingualism in the dominant language. Usually, any minority language whose speakers were highly bilingual in a dominant language was classed as endangered as its speakers are likely to shift to the dominant language.
- The prevalence of socio-political factors that put pressure on the minority language. In some cases historical or political factors may exert pressure or place the minority language speakers in a state of dependence, inducing a shift to the dominant language.
- Socio-economic disadvantage of the minority language speakers. Where these were socio-economically vulnerable or dependent on the dominant language speakers, it was assumed that the former will be attracted to the language of the more powerful group.
- The prevalence of negative attitudes towards their language. Where minority language speakers no longer saw value in their language, it was taken as an indicator of language endangerment
- Non-transmission of the minority language to the younger generation. Where parents no longer taught their children the minority language but instead encouraged them to learn the dominant language, this was taken as a clear indicator of language endangerment.
- Situations where only people beyond child-bearing age spoke the minority language. This was taken as a clear indication of a highly endangered language.

As not all the information was available in a number of cases, some languages may have been erroneously included in or left out of the list of highly endangered languages that follows. Although we relied mainly on Grimes (2000) for the number of languages in each country, the numbers have been adjusted to exclude dialects, non-creolised pidgins and extinct languages. The figures for the population of each country are based on Katzner (2002). The size stated for each country is an indication of its geographical extent. For information on the extinct or nearly extinct languages we have made use of various sources, including Grimes (2000), Wurm (1996), UNESCO (2003a), Sommer (1992), Haarmann (2001), Mann and Dalby (1987) and other individual or personal sources. In the listing of the names of languages, names linked by a hyphen indicate a language cluster that is regarded as one linguistic entity, while those given in brackets are alternative names.

(1) Algeria

Algeria is a large country with a population of over 30 million people. It has 15 languages, of which Arabic is the official/national language and also the nationally dominant language. It is spoken by more than two-thirds of the population. Kabyle, spoken in the mountains east of Algiers, is the only major areally dominant language.

There are many small, scattered Berber language clusters. The most endangered include Tamacine–Tamazighe, Tidikelt–Tamazighe and Korandje. All three appear to be giving way to Arabic.

(2) Angola

Angola is a medium-sized country with a population of over 11 million people. There are 39 languages including the official language, Portuguese. The three major areally dominant languages are Umbundu in the central area, Kimbundu (Luanda) in the north, and Kikongo in the far north. All are of Bantu origin.

The highly endangered languages include Nyendo, Kung-Ekoka, Maligo and !Kung. Kwadi and Kwisi are already extinct.

(3) Benin

Benin is a small country with a population of about six million people. It has 48 languages, with French as the official/national language. The four major areally dominant languages are Fon-Gbe in the south, Yoruba along the eastern border, and Hausa and Bariba in the north.

The highly endangered languages include Aguna, Basa, Boulba, Anii (Gisida) and Anufo (Chokosi). All of them have few speakers, who are bilingual in one of the areally dominant languages. The only reported extinct language is Tyanda (Sommer, 1992).

(4) Botswana

Botswana is a medium-sized country with a population of around 1.7 million people. It has 28 languages, of which English and Setswana are the official and national languages, respectively. Setswana is also the nationally dominant language, spoken by 78.6% of the population as first language and by a total of over 90% as both first and second language. The only major areally dominant language is Ikalanga, spoken by over 150,000 people in the northeast of the country.

The highly endangered languages include Kua, Shua, Tshwa, |Gwi, ||Gana, ‡Kx'au||'ein, ‡Hua and some of the varieties of Khwedam, namely,

‖Ani, |Anda and Buga. All are Khoesan languages, most with fewer than 2000 speakers. Many are spoken in scattered clusters, which makes them more vulnerable. The highly endangered Bantu languages include Shiyeyi, Sebirwa and Setswapong. All these languages are highly influenced by Setswana. The extinct languages are Deti-Khwe and Gabake-Ntshori (Grimes, 2000).

(5) Burkina Faso

Burkina Faso is a medium-sized country with a population of about 12 million people. There are 55 languages, with French as the official language. The nationally dominant language is Mossi-More, while the three major areally dominant languages are Dyula, Fulfude and Gurmanche. All are used extensively as second languages.

The highly endangered languages include Ble, Khe (Kheso), Khisa (Komono), Natioro, Sininkere (Silunde), Tiefo, Wara and Zarma. These not only have few speakers, but their speakers are also highly bilingual in the dominant languages. The extinct or nearly extinct languages are Noumoudara-Koumoudam (a dialect of Tiefo) and Jelkuna (Sommer, 1992).

(6) Burundi

Burundi is geographically very small but densely populated, with a population of over six million people. Three languages are spoken in the country, of which French is the official language and Kirundi the national and nationally dominant language. The only other language is Kiswahili, which is used mainly in urban centres as a commercial language. There are no records of extinct languages.

(7) Cameroon

Cameroon is a medium-sized country with a population of more than 14 million. With 274 languages, it is one of the countries in Africa with a high concentration of languages. Hence, there are many instances of language contact, bilingualism and dominance patterns, which have caused many languages to become highly endangered or even extinct.

There is no nationally dominant language. However, there are a number of major areally dominant languages, which include Pidgin English, Fulfude, Ewondo (Bulu) and Duala. In fact, Pidgin English is the lingua franca in southern Cameroon, spoken by at least half of the Cameroonian population as a second language.

The highly endangered languages include Akum, Bakole, Bangandu, Barombi, Bati (Batiba Ngong), Bubia (Bobe), Buduma, Dimbong, Eman, Evant, Gyele, Hijuk, Isu, Kendem, Kolbila, Mampai, To, Tuotamb, Twendi,

Yukuberi and Zizilivakan. All these are used by small numbers of speakers, who are highly bilingual in the areally dominant languages. Moreover, a number of languages are extinct or nearly extinct. These are Bikya, Bishuo, Bung, Busuu, Duli, Gey (Gueve), Nagumi (Bama), Ndai, Ngang, Yeni, Zumaya, Luo, Galke, Homa, Isuwu, Kole, Mboa, Mbong, Befon, Bonek, Ehobe and Poko.

(8) Canary Islands
The Canary Islands are a group of small islands off the Senegalese coast, constituting an autonomous territory of Spain with a population of just over one million people. The only currently spoken language in the archipelago is Spanish. Apparently, a Berber language known as Guanche became extinct on the islands in the 16th century (Grimes, 2000).

(9) Cape Verde
This is an archipelago of small islands inhabited by about 400,000 people. Two languages are spoken, including the official language, Portuguese. The other language is a creole, known as Kabuverdianu (Caboverdiano), which is the commonly used lingua franca. There are no records of extinct languages.

(10) Central African Republic
The Central African Republic is a medium-sized country with a population of over three million people. It has 53 languages, of which French is the official language. The nationally dominant and widely used language is Sango. However, there are two major areally dominant languages, Gbaya in the west and Banda in the central and eastern parts of the country.
The highly endangered languages are Ali and Geme. Although Ali is spoken by a sizable number of people, it is losing ground to Sango as most children are learning Sango as a first language (Grimes, 2000: 56). There are two extinct or nearly extinct languages, Bodo and Birri.

(11) Chad
Chad is a large country with a population of about eight million people. There are 126 languages, of which French and standard Arabic are the official languages. The major areally dominant languages are Chadic Arabic, spoken mainly in the north, and Sara and Ngambay, which are widely used in the south.
The highly endangered languages include Barein, Boor (Bowara, Damraw), Fania (Mara, Kobe, Fongoro, Koke), Kindeje (Yaali), Kujange, Laal, Mawa (Mahoura), Miltu, Saba, Sokoro, Tamki, Tunia (Tounia, Tunya)

and Zan Gula (Moriil). The extinct or nearly extinct languages are Berakou, Buso (Dam de Bouso), Gourdo, Horo (Hor), Massalat, Muskum, Niellim, Sokoro, Noy, Amdang, Ndam and Sarwa.

(12) Comoro Islands

The Comoro Islands are an archipelago of three small islands (if one excludes Mayotte) in the Indian Ocean with a population of about 700,000. Six languages are spoken, with French and Arabic as the official/national languages. Comorian Kiswahili, known as Shingazidja, is the commonly used language.

The other languages are Shindzwani and Shimaore, spoken in the smaller islands, and Madagascar. The first two could be considered as varieties of Shingazidja. Both appear to be giving way to the latter.

(13) Congo Republic

The People's Republic of Congo is a medium-sized country with a population of over 2.5 million people. There are 53 languages, of which French is the official language. The nationally dominant language is Monokotuba, a creolised form of Kikongo. The only major areally dominant language is Lingala, spoken mainly in the north of the country.

Since most languages are spoken by scattered communities in remote areas, language contact or dominance is not so pronounced. Hence, cases of language endangerment are few. In fact, from our survey no language appears to be highly threatened. However, with the growing national importance of Monokotuba many minority languages will probably become threatened. There is therefore a need to conduct a systematic investigation of the patterns of language domination in the country. The extinct or nearly extinct languages include Barambu, Boguru, Mangbele, Fumu and Ngbinda.

(14) Côte d'Ivoire

Côte d'Ivoire is a medium-sized country with a population of about 15 million. It has 58 languages, of which French is the official language. The major areally dominant languages are Anyi-Baule, which is widely spoken in the south, and Dyula and Senoufo in the north.

The highly endangered languages include Beti (Eotile), Daho-Doo, Ega (Dies) and Kodia (Kwadya). The extinct or nearly extinct languages are Esuma, Dungi (Dungu) and Ligbi.

(15) Democratic Republic of Congo

The Democratic Republic of Congo is a large country with a population of about 50 million. It has 209 languages, with French as the official language.

The major areally dominant languages are Kikongo in the west, Lingala in the northwest, Luba-Katanga in the southeast and Kiswahili in the east. These languages are also known as provincial languages as they are widely used as second languages or linguae francae in their respective areas.

Highly endangered languages include Beeke (Beke), Bolondo, Bomboli, Gbanziri, Kwami (Khwami), Lonzo, Monzombo, Yango (Gbendere) and Dzando. The extinct or nearly extinct languages are Dongoko, Kazibati, Mampoko, Mbondo, Mongoba and Ngbee. There is a need to investigate the status of many of the languages as information is still scanty.

(16) Djibouti

Djibouti is a small country with a population of just over 500,000. There are four languages including French, the official language. The others are Afar (Afaraf, Dasakil), spoken by more than half the population, and Somali and Arabic, which are also widely spoken. None of the languages is threatened.

(17) Egypt

Egypt is a relatively large country with a population of over 65 million. It has six languages, of which standard Arabic is the official/national language. Arabic, in its different varieties, is also the nationally dominant language, spoken by more than 97% of the population.

The relatively endangered languages include Kenuzi-Dongola, of Nubian origin, and Sini (Siwa), of Berber origin. The extinct languages are Coptic, a language of the Egyptian sub-family, which is presumed to have become extinct in the 16th century, and Ge'ez. Both are still in use as largely liturgical languages.

(18) Equatorial Guinea

Equatorial Guinea is a very small country with a population of about 500,000. There are 13 languages, of which Spanish is the official language. Fang is the nationally dominant language, spoken by more than 75% of the population.

There are no conspicuously endangered languages, nor records of extinct languages.

(19) Eritrea

Eritrea is a very small country with a population of about four million. It has 11 languages, of which English is the official/national language. The two major areally dominant languages are Tigrinya and Tigre, both of Semitic origin. Arabic is also widely spoken as a second language.

The only highly endangered language is Bilen (Bogo, Bileng). Ge'ez (Ancient Ethiopic) has become extinct, and as in Egypt is used only in liturgical services.

(20) Ethiopia
Ethiopia is a large country with a population of about 63 million people. There are 78 languages in the country, including the official/national languages Amharic, Tigrinya and English. The nationally dominant language is Amharic, which has been accorded a privileged position and high social status. The major areally dominant languages include Oromo, Tigrinya and Somali. All are spoken by a considerable number of second-language speakers.

The highly endangered languages include Anfillo, Bambassi, Kano, Kwama (Gongwama), Ometo, Saho, Opuuo (Cita, Kwira), Seze and Zay (Lak'í). The languages which have become extinct or are nearly extinct are Argobba, Bayso, Burji, Gafat, Ganza (Ganzo, Koma), Rer Bare (Berebere, Adona), Agaw (western variety), Weyto, Kwegu (Bacha, Menja), Birale (Angota), Gatame, Ganjule, Qwarenya, Gomba, Kimanteney (Quara, K'emant), Shabo, Omo-Murle and Xamtang'a. Additionally, Ge'ez is used as a liturgical language but not in everyday communication.

(21) Gabon
Gabon is a small country with a population of just over one million people. It has 40 languages, of which French is the official language. The only major areally dominant language is Fang, which is spoken by at least 40% of the population, though mainly in the north of the country.

The highly endangered languages include Kande (Kanda), Pinji, Seki (Sekiani) and Simba. There are no records of extinct or nearly extinct languages.

(22) Gambia
Gambia is a very small country with a population of just over one million. It has nine languages, of which English is the official language. The major areally dominant language is Mandinka (Malinke), spoken mainly in the west of the country.

The only language which appears to be highly endangered at present is Kalanke. There are no records of extinct or nearly extinct languages.

(23) Ghana
Ghana is a medium-sized country with a population of about 20 million. It has 76 languages, with English as the official language. The major areally

dominant languages are Akan (Asante, Twi, Fante and Akwapem), spoken by 44% of the Ghanaian population but used mainly in the south, Ewe and Ga-Adangme in the southeast, and Dagbane in the north.

The highly endangered languages include Chakali, Chala, Dompo (Dumpo, Ndambo), Dwang, Hanga, Kamara, Kantosi and Nchumbulu. The only known extinct language in Ghana is Boro.

(24) Guinea

Guinea is a medium-sized country with a population of about eight million people. There are 23 languages, with French as the official language. The major areally dominant languages are Fuuta Jalon (Fulfude, Pulaar), which is spoken in the central part, Mandinka (Malinke) in the north, and Susu in the southwest. The highly endangered languages include Baga Binari, Baga Mandun and Baga Mtoteni. Three languages are known to be extinct or nearly extinct: Baga Kaloum, Baga Koga and Baga Sobane (Burka, Sobane).

(25) Guinea-Bissau

Guinea-Bissau is a very small country with a population of just over one million. It has 20 languages, of which Portuguese is the official language. The nationally dominant language is Crioulo (Portuguese Creole), which is spoken as first or second language by over 70% of the population. The major areally dominant languages are Balanta and Pulaar (Fulfude).

The highly endangered languages are Badjara, Kasanga (Cassanga, Haal) and Kobiana. There is only one reported extinct or nearly extinct language, namely Buy.

(26) Kenya

Kenya is a medium-sized country with a population of about 30 million people. Of the 56 languages, English is the official language and Kiswahili is the national language. Kiswahili, spoken mainly as a second language, is the nationally dominant language. The major areally dominant languages are Gikuyu in the central highlands, Luo around Lake Victoria in the west, Kikamba in the east and Luyia in the far west.

The highly endangered languages include Boni, Dahalo, Burji (Bambala), Daasanach, Digo, Konkani (Goanese), Malakote (Ilwana), Nubi (Kinubi), Sagalla (Teri), Sanye and Suba, as well as Chifundi and Vumba (both Kiswahili dialects). The extinct or nearly extinct languages are Elmolo (El Molo), Okiek (Akiek, Ndorobo), Yaaku (Mukodogo, Ndorobo), Omotik (Laamot, Ndorobo), Kore, Bong'om, Degere, Kinare, Lorkoti, Segeju, Sogoo and Ware.

(27) Lesotho
Lesotho is a very small country with a population of just over two million. The two languages are English, used as the official language, and Sesotho, the only indigenous language. There are, however, pockets of minority languages of Nguni origin and languages spoken by immigrant groups. One of the latter, known as Seroa, has become extinct.

(28) Liberia
Liberia is a small country with a population of about three million. It has 23 languages, of which English is the official language. The major areally dominant languages are Liberian Pidgin English, spoken mainly as a second language, Kpelle in the east, and Bassa in the central parts near the coast.
There are two highly endangered languages, Gbii and Dewoin (Dey). There is no record of an extinct or nearly extinct language.

(29) Libya
Libya is a relatively large country with a population of just over five million. Of the seven languages, Arabic is the official/national language. Arabic is also the nationally dominant language, spoken by 96% of the population. The other indigenous languages are mainly of Berber origin.
The highly endangered languages include Awjilah (Augila), Domari and Ghadames. Sawkrah (Sokra) is reported to be extinct or nearly extinct.

(30) Madagascar
Madagascar, an island off the eastern coast in the Indian Ocean, has a population of just over 15 million people. Four languages are spoken, with French as the official language and Malagasy as the national language. Malagasy is also the nationally dominant language, spoken by more than 90% of the population.
The only minority language in the island is Comorian Kiswahili, spoken by about 25,000 people. However, the language is highly vibrant and maintains itself well.

(31) Malawi
Malawi is a small country with a population of over 10 million people. There are 15 languages, with English as the official language. The nationally dominant language is Chinyanja (Chichewa), which for a long time enjoyed high prestige and social status. The other major areally dominant languages are Chiyao and Chitumbuka.
The only highly endangered language is Malawian Ngoni, whose speakers are shifting to Chichewa/Chinyanja.

(32) Mali
Mali is a large country with a population of more than 10 million. It has 28 languages, including French as the official language. The nationally dominant language is Bambara (Manding), spoken by the majority of the people as first or second language. The major areally dominant languages are Fulfude, Songhay Senoufo and Soninke.

The highly endangered languages include Bankagoma (Banka), Pana (Sama) and Samoma. The extinct or nearly extinct languages include the original language of the Jahanka (related to Soninke), Azer and Kakolo.

(33) Mauritania
Mauritania is a medium-sized country with a population of just over two and a half million people. It has six languages, of which Arabic is the official/national language. The nationally dominant language is Hassaniyya, an Arabic creole spoken by the majority of the people as first or second language. There are two highly endangered languages, Imeraguen (a variety of Hassaniyya) and Zenaga.

(34) Mauritius
Mauritius is a small island in the Indian Ocean with a population of about one million people. Six languages are spoken, including English as the official language. The nationally dominant languages are Morisyen (Mauritius Creole), spoken by the majority of the people as first or second language. The only major areally dominant language is Bhojpuri. There are no obviously endangered languages on the island.

(35) Mayotte
Mayotte, a small island that was formerly part of the Comoro archipelago, has a population of about 100,000. Four languages are spoken in the island, of which French is the official language. Shimaore, a variety of Comorian, is the main indigenous language.

The only visibly endangered language is Kiswahili, which is used by just over 2000 people who are bilingual in Shimaore. However, the variety of Kiswahili found in Mayotte is significantly different from that spoken elsewhere in eastern Africa.

(36) Morocco
Morocco is a medium-sized country with a population of about 30 million people. There are seven languages, of which standard Arabic is the official language. Arabic is also the nationally dominant language, spoken by over 70% of the population. The other languages are mainly of Berber origin but also include French and Spanish.

There are no visibly endangered languages, but there are two extinct languages, Ghomara and Senhaja de Srair (Sanhaja of Srair).

(37) Mozambique

Mozambique is a medium-sized country with a population of about 20 million. The 33 languages include Portuguese as the official language. The major areally dominant languages are Emakhua (with its varieties Elomwe and Cuabo) in the north and Tsonga in the south. Portuguese is also extensively spoken as a second language.

The highly endangered languages include Tekela (Mozambican Siswati) and Sunda (Mozambican Zulu). Language shift in the case of these languages will depend largely on in-migration from the main group sources. (The term in-migration denotes migration into the areas from the main sources of the relevant speakers, in this case the Siswati and IsiZulu speakers of South Africa and Swaziland.) The other highly endangered language is Shichopi, spoken in the southern part of the country.

(38) Namibia

Namibia is a medium-sized country with a population of just over one and a half million. It has 26 languages, of which English is the official language. All the indigenous languages are designated as national languages in the country's language policy. However, Afrikaans is the actively used lingua franca, particularly in urban areas and the southern parts of the country. Although Oshiwambo (including Oshikwanyama, Oshidonga and Oshikwambi) is spoken by over 50% of the population, it has not established itself as a nationally dominant language. It remains, therefore, a major areally dominant language.

The highly endangered languages include !Aakhoe ǂKx'au‖'ein, Kung-Ekoka, !Kung, Hai‖'om, Mashi and Shiyeyi. Two languages, ǂKhomani and !Ora (Kora), have become extinct.

(39) Niger

Niger is a medium-sized country with a population of about 10 million. There are 13 languages including the official language, French. The nationally dominant language is Hausa, spoken by the majority of the people as first or second language. The major areally dominant language is Djerma (Zarma), in the southwest. The highly endangered languages are Tedaga (Tebu) and Tasawa (Ingelshi). There is no record of any extinct language.

(40) Nigeria

Nigeria is a medium-sized country with a high population density. The population is about 120 million. There are 485 languages in the country, of which English is the official language. The major areally dominant languages are Hausa in the north, Yoruba in the southwest and Igbo in the southeast.

The large number of endangered and extinct or nearly extinct languages for Nigeria is largely due to the fact that the country has one of the highest concentrations of languages in the world. Thus, there are many incidences of language contact, bilingualism, dominance and language shift (Blench, 1998). Moreover, Nigeria has not only the highest number and density of languages in Africa but also the most complex language situation. It is also a country with conspicuous language inequality, ranging from the dominant languages Hausa, Yoruba and Igbo, each with at least 20 million speakers (together accounting for more than two–thirds of the population) to very small languages each spoken by scarcely 100 people (Katzner, 2002: 357).

The highly endangered languages include Abon (Abong, Ba'ban), Ahan (Ahaan), Ake (Akye), Alege (Alegi, Uge, Ugbe), Ambo, Bali (Bibaali, Maya), Beele (Bele, Bellawa), Bina (Bogana, Binawa), Bure (Bubure), Buru, Cara (Caara, Nfachara), Ciwaga, Cori (Chori), Daba (Dabba), Defaka (Afakani), Dendi (Dandawa), Doka, Duhwa (Karfa, Kerifa, Nzuhwi), Dulbu, Dungu (Dungi, Dunjawa), Dwai (Enji, Eastern Bode), Eruwa (Erohwa, Erakwa), Fam, Firan (Faran, Foron), Fungwa (Tufungwa, Ura, Ula), Gyem (Gyemawa, Gema), Hasha (Yashi), Horom, Hungworo (Ngwoi, Nkwoi, Ingwe), Idon, Iyive (Uive, Ndir, Asumbo), Janji (Anafejanzi, Jijanji), Jilbe (Zoulbou), Jimi (Bi-Gimu), Ju, Kaivi (Kaibi), Kariya (Kauyawa), Kiphawa (Vinahe, Wihe), Kinuku (Kinuka), Korenoem (Kanam), Kono (Kowono), Kubi (Kuba, Kubawa), Kugbo, Kutto (Kupto), Kuturmi (Ada), Luri, Maghdi (Tala, Widala), Mala (Rumaya, Tumala), Mangas, Mashi, Mbogno (Kakaba, Kamkam), Mingang Doso (Munga Doso), Mundat, Mvanip (Magu), Ndunda, Nggwahyi, Ningye, Nkukoli (Lokoli, Ekuri), Piti (Pitti, Abisi), Ruma (Ruruma, Bagwama), Sha, Shiki (Gubi, Guba, Mashiki), Shuwa-Zamani (Kuzamani, Rishuwa, Kauru), Somyiwe (Kila), Surubu (Fiti), Tala, Tha (Joole Marga, Kapawa), Tumi (Tutumi, Kitimi), Vono (Kiwollo), Wase (Jukun Wase), Yangkam (Yankam, Basharawa, Bashar) and Zangwal (Zwangal, Twar).

The extinct or nearly extinct languages are Ajawa (Aja, Ajanci), Basa-Gumna (Basa-Kaduna, Basa-Kuta), Bete, Centum (Cen Tum), Auyokama, Bade, Bassa-Kantagora, Faliof, Baissa, Gana, Holma (Da Holmaci, Bali Holma), Kiong (Akayon, Akoiyang, Iyoniyong), Bissaula, Lere, Lufu, Mawa, Njerep (Njerup), Odut, Putai (Margli West), Sheni (Shani, Shaiwi), Kpan, Kpati, Taura, Tesherawa, Ziriya, Agara'iwa, Cena, Chamo, Gamo, Gubi, Gwara, Izora, Kiballo, Kir, Kudu, Nimbari, Ningi, Pishi, Shanga, Shau, Shirawa, Taura, Tijanji and Yashi.

(41) Rwanda
Rwanda is a very small but densely populated country. The population is about 7.5 million. Four languages are spoken, of which French is the main official language. Kinyarwanda is the only indigenous language. The other languages are Kiswahili, spoken mainly in urban centres as a commercial language, and English, which has been adopted as a co-official language with French. There is no endangered language or record of extinct languages in the country.

(42) São Tomé è Principe
São Tomé è Principe is a small country, part of which is an island off the coast of Gabon. The population is about 150,000. Four languages are spoken, including Portuguese as the official language. The nationally dominant language is Saotomense, a Portuguese creole, which has become the commonly used language in the country. There is neither a visibly endangered language nor any record of extinct languages.

(43) Senegal
Senegal is a medium-sized country with a population of about 10 million. There are 34 languages, of which the official language is French. Wolof, spoken as first or second language by 87% of the population, is the nationally dominant language. The other major areally dominant languages are Fulfude and Serer-Sine.
The highly endangered languages include Bandjana (Badyara, Pajadinka, Gola), Bainouk-Samik and Kobiana (Uboi, Buy). There are two extinct or nearly extinct languages, Bedik and Haal.

(44) Seychelles
The Seychelles is a country consisting of a group of islands in the Indian Ocean inhabited by about 80,000 people. Three languages are spoken, of which English and French are the official languages. The third is Seselwa, a creole, also known as Seychelles Creole or Seychellois, spoken by the majority of the people in non-formal situations. There is no endangered language or record of extinct languages.

(45) Sierra Leone
Sierra Leone is a small country with a population of about five million. It has 22 languages, of which English is the official language. The nationally dominant language is Krio, an English creole used as a lingua franca. The major areally dominant languages are Mende in the south-central area and Temne in the northwest.

There are two endangered languages, Bom (Bome, Bomo) and Krim (Kim, Kiltim, Kirim, Kimi). The extinct or nearly extinct languages are Bullom So (Bolem), Banta and Dama.

(46) Somalia

Somalia is a medium-sized country with a population of over seven million people. There are 12 languages including Somali, which is the official/national language. Somali is also the nationally dominant language, spoken by the majority of the people. However, there are pockets of other languages.

The highly endangered languages include Chimiini (Bravanese) and Bajuni (both remote varieties of Kiswahili), as well as Garre (Af-Garre), Mushungulu (Mmushungulu) and Tunni (Af-Tunni). There is only one nearly extinct language, namely Boni, also known as Boon (Af-Boon). Although still spoken in Kenya, this language is highly endangered.

(47) South Africa

South Africa is a large country with a population of about 42 million. The 23 languages include 11 with official status: Afrikaans, English, Sindebele, Sepedi, Sesotho, Siswati, Shitsonga, Setswana, IsiXhosa, IsiZulu and Tshivenda. The major areally dominant languages are IsiZulu, IsiXhosa, Afrikaans, Setswana and Sesotho. English, as an ex-colonial language, is widely used in education and government business.

The highly endangered languages include Camtho (IsiCamtho), Sebowa, Gail and Kxoe (Mbarahuesa, Mbarakwengo). Moreover, there are many extinct languages, most of Khoesan origin, which became extinct largely during the time of Bantu and Dutch settlements in southern Africa several centuries ago. They include Korana (!Ora, !Kora), N|u, |Xam, ||Xegwi, Xiri (Criqua, Cape Hottentot), Seroa and Gemsbok Nama.

(48) Sudan

Sudan is a large country with a population of about 32 million. It has 121 languages, of which Arabic is the official/national language. The major areally dominant languages are Arabic (Sudanese Creole or Juba Arabic), spoken mainly in the north, and Dinka, spoken mainly in the south.

The highly endangered languages include Aja (Ajja, Adja), Aka, Bai (Bari), Baygo (Baigo, Bego), Boguru, Dair (Daier, Thaminyi), El Hugeirat, Logol (Lukfa), Logorik (Liguri), Mangayat (Mangaya, Bug), Mo'da (Gberi, Gweri, Muda), Molo (Malkan, Tara-ka-Molo), Njalgulgule (Nyolge, Bege, Beko), Nyamusa-Molo, Suri (Surma), Talodi (Gajo-Mang, Jomang), Tese (Teis-umm-Danab, Keiga, Jirru), Tima (Lomorik, Lomuriki, Tamanik, Yibwa), Wali (Walari, Walarishe) and Warnang (Werni).

The extinct or nearly extinct languages are Berti, Gule (Anej, Hamej, Fecakomoliyo), Homa, Togoyo (Togoy), Torona, Birked, Fongoro, Jur Modo, Kello, Mittu, Morokodo, Birgid, Bodo, Buga, Eliri, Haraza, Kidie (Lafofa), Kreish, Meroitic, Ngbinda, Tagbu, Tenet and Wetu.

Sudan has many endangered and extinct languages because of the high concentration of languages, particularly in the Nile region, and its marked political instability, which has caused many population movements.

(49) Swaziland

Swaziland is a small country with a population of about one million. There are four languages, of which English is the official language. Siswati is the nationally dominant language. The other languages are Shitsonga and IsiZulu, spoken where the country borders on South Africa and Mozambique. There are no endangered languages or records of extinct languages.

(50) Tanzania

Tanzania is a medium-sized country with a population of 35 million. It has 124 languages, with Kiswahili as the main official and national language and English as the second official language, mainly in higher education and international dealings. Kiswahili is also the nationally dominant language, spoken by over 90% of the population as first or second language. The only major areally dominant language is Kisukuma, which is spoken in the northern part of the country by more than 12.5% of the population.

The highly endangered languages include Daiso (Dhaiso), Gweno (Kigweno), Hadza (Hadzapi, Kitindiga), Akie (Ndorobo, Kisankara), Kwavi (Parakuyo), Bondei, Doe, Burunge, Gorowa, Holoholo, Ikizu, Ikoma, Isanzu, Jiji, Kabwa, Kami, Kisi, Makwe, Manda, Mbungwe, Segeju (Sageju), Nghwele, Pimbwe, Rungwe, Suba, Alagwa (Wasi, Asi), Vidunda, Vinza, Zinza, Surwa, Sweta, Wanda and Zalamo (Zaramo). The extinct or nearly extinct languages are Aasax (Asax, Asak), Ongamo (Ngasa), Kikae (Old Kimakunduchi), Kw'adza, Degere, Yeke, Hamba, Bahi and Ware.

The high rate of language endangerment and extinction in Tanzania is mainly a result of the dominance of Kiswahili as both official and national language (Batibo, 1992). The enormous prestige and power which it has accumulated is exerting irresistible pressure on most of the minority languages in the country.

(51) Togo

Togo is a very small country with a population of about five million. The 42 languages include French as the official language. There are two major areally dominant languages, Ewe (Krepe, Popo) in the south, and Kabiye

(Kabre, Kabye) in the north. The highly endangered languages include Sola (Soruba, Biyobe, Solamba), Kpesi, Igo (Ago, Ahonlan), Bissa and Bago. There is no record of extinct or nearly extinct languages.

(52) Tunisia

Tunisia is a small country with a population of about 10 million people. It has four languages, of which Arabic is the official language. It is also the nationally dominant language, spoken by 96% of the population.

There is no highly endangered language, but there are two extinct languages, Sened (a Berber language) and Sabir (a Petit Mauresque port pidgin).

(53) Uganda

Uganda is a small country with a population of about 23 million. It has 34 languages, with English as the official language. There are two major areally dominant languages, Luganda, spoken mainly in the south, and Kiswahili, spoken as a second language in many parts of the country, particularly in urban centres.

There are only two highly endangered languages, namely Ik (Ngulak) and Soo (So, Tepes). The extinct or nearly extinct languages are Nyang'i (Nyangeya, Nyangia), Singa (Lusinga), Kooki and Napore.

(54) Zambia

Zambia is a medium-sized country with a population of about 10 million. Its 38 languages include English as the official language. The major areally dominant languages are Chibemba in the north, Chinyanja in the east-central region and Chitonga in the south.

There are only two highly endangered languages, Mbowe (Esimbowe) and Yauma. The only extinct or nearly extinct language is the Zambian varieties of Kxoe, now known as Khwedam in its grouping with other related languages.

(55) Zimbabwe

Zimbabwe is a medium-sized country with a population of just over 11 million. There are 17 languages, of which English is the official language and Chishona the national language. Chishona, spoken by nearly 80% of the population, is also the nationally dominant language. Sindebele is a major areally dominant language, particularly in the southwest.

There are two highly endangered languages, Hietshware (Hiechware, Tshwa) and Dombe (Grimes, 2000). There is no record of extinct languages apart from ||Xegwi, which may once have been spoken in some parts of the country.

A general scenario of language endangerment and death in Africa

It is clear from the above country-by-country case studies that the problem of language endangerment and death is a real one in Africa. As shown in Appendix 3, which summarises the situation of language endangerment and death in the continent, of a total of 2193 languages currently spoken (according to our survey), 308 are highly endangered and 201 are extinct or nearly extinct. This means that 14.0% are highly endangered and 8.3% are extinct or nearly extinct. This scenario is, in fact, only the tip of the iceberg, given that not only do we not have complete socio-linguistic information for most of these languages, but also the momentum of language shift may accelerate with increased pressure from the dominant languages, whose prestige and power are growing as they assume national roles. As can be seen from Appendix 3, there is a great imbalance in terms of language distribution country by country, the number of endangered and extinct or nearly extinct languages in each country, and the number of dominant languages. Usually, the most lethal language-killers are the nationally dominant and the major areally dominant languages. Hence, the 1623 languages that have been listed as less endangered or relatively safe may not be safe enough to ensure their survival over the course of this century.

Summary and Conclusions

An endangered language is a language that is threatened by extinction. Endangerment is relative as some languages are more threatened than others. There are, however, certain indicators that characterise such a language. Normally, endangerment occurs when a weaker language is unable to sustain the pressure from a stronger language or if speakers of the former decide to give in as part of a strategy of integration into the stronger or larger language community.

A number of surveys have been carried out on the languages of Africa, ranging from those which have considered the whole continent to more restricted studies dealing with regions, countries or individual languages. The crucial question in most of these surveys has been how to determine when a given language is truly endangered. As different criteria have been used, the surveys have yielded different results. So far, the most extensive set of studies are those which have been carried out by the Summer Institute of Linguistics (SIL), published under the name *Ethnologue*, which provides vital information on most of the languages of the world.

It is gratifying to note, however, that research on endangered languages has increased rapidly in recent years, although there remains considerable imbalance in its distribution. A number of organisations and foundations are beginning to show interest and to provide material support for such research. At the same time, the number of both foreign and local scholars interested in the question of language endangerment and death in Africa is growing rapidly.

Chapter 6

Language Shift and Death in Africa

Definitions of Language Shift and Language Death

In current sociolinguistic studies the terms *language shift* and *language death* are used as metaphors. *Language shift* results when speakers abandon their language, willingly or under pressure, in favour of another language, which then takes over as their means of communication and socialisation. *Language death* refers to the state of extinction, that is, the language is no longer used as a means of communication or socialisation. Language death may occur through the abandonment of a language by its speakers, the non-use of the language in any domain, the disappearance of its speakers or the non-functioning of its structure. The processes of language shift and language death are interrelated as usually a language becomes extinct when its speakers shift to another language. However, a language can also become extinct if all its speakers are eliminated, for example by genocide.

Major Theoretical Perspectives on Language Shift and Death

A number of theoretical approaches have been proposed to capture the process whereby an endangered language is progressively reduced to extinction or how its speakers shift to another language. There are two major types of approach. One considers the set of factors and circumstances that cause or attend the abandonment by a language group of its language in favour of another; these are: when it allows itself, or is forced by certain circumstances, to be absorbed into another language group; reduction in the domains of use of a language; and loss of a group's loyalty to its language. The theory also looks at the structural changes affecting a language that is moving towards extinction.

The second type of theoretical approach has concerned itself with the processes involved in language shift and death. It focuses on the various stages that a language goes through on its way to extinction and the way it progressively loses its domains of use on the one hand, and its stylistic and structural complexity on the other. The two approaches are, of course, complementary as they consider two aspects of the same problem. Models based on the first approach are known as *causality-based models* and those based on the second approach are known as *process-based models*.

In the next sections we shall examine two models of language shift and death that are based on the two approaches, both of which have been found to be relevant to the African situation.

The causality-based perspective

Under the causality-based perspective we are going to consider a well-known model, the Gaelic–Arvanitika model (GAM). This model, established by Hans-Jürgen Sasse (1992), originated from two case studies. One was on the Arvanitika language of Greece and the other was on the East Sutherland variety of Scottish Gaelic. The model is based on three types of phenomena relevant to the process of language death. The first is the entire range of extra-linguistic factors: cultural, sociological, ethno-historical and economic. Many of these factors coincide with those proposed by Edwards (1992) in his studies of language vitality. Such factors create in a speech community a situation of pressure to give up its language. This phenomenon is known in the GAM model as the *external setting*. The external setting acts as a catalyst to the process of language death as it triggers the existence of the other phenomena. The second set of phenomena is termed as *speech behaviour*. This refers to the use of variables that are usually determined by social parameters, such as language choice, choice of register, domains of use, language attitudes and so on. Since the political and social conditions are primary in any speech community, the phenomena of the external setting have a strong impact on speech behaviour.

The third type of phenomena involves structural changes resulting from the pressure and the speakers' response to it. These changes could be in the sound system, morphological structure, syntactic rules or lexicon of the language threatened by extinction. This set of phenomena is referred to in the model as *structural consequences*. So, to sum up, the GAM model involves three areas of study: extra-linguistic (political, sociological, ethnographical, socio-economic, etc.); sociolinguistic (language choice, choice of register, domains of use, language attitudes); and structural linguistic (phonological, morphological, syntactic, semantic and lexical).

According to the Gaelic–Arvanitika model, the three sets of phenomena form an implicational chain: the phenomena of the external setting induce a certain kind of speech behaviour, which in turn results in certain structural alterations in the dying language. Normally this cause–effect chain of events starts when a speech community becomes bilingual such that one language, the *abandoned language*, is gradually abandoned in favour of another, the *target language*. According to the model, the primary language shift is initiated at the sociolinguistic level – specifically, when a speech community ceases to transmit its language to its descendants. The result is an interruption in *language transmission*. The interruption of transmission could be a result of the weaker position of the speakers socio-economically or demographically, inducing them to choose to use the target language. Also, because the recessive abandoned language is less and less able to deal with certain domains, the target dominant language progressively becomes the main language. The process of language recession reaches a point of *language decay*, that is, a serious linguistic disintegration, which is typical of the speech of the so-called 'semi-speakers'. Since transmission is suppressed, it becomes highly imperfect and even scanty. There tends to be a defective morphology, pidgin-like simplification and an extremely limited lexicon. Finally, the language is no longer transmissible. It is dead.

The pertinence of the GAM model to this study is its emphasis on the factors that trigger the process of language shift. As seen above, a language becomes highly endangered when certain external factors arise, such as political domination, economic dependence, cultural infiltration, historical legacies or social inequality. These factors impact on the speakers' attitudes and behaviour towards their language. The consequence of this situation is the gradual abandonment of a language, which at the same time under-goes progressive structural reduction.

The process-based perspective

The model we are going to present under the process-based perspective is known as the 'marked bilingualism model'. This was propounded by the present author (Batibo, 1992, 1997), following his language surveys in Tanzania and Botswana. It is based on the following assumptions:

- language shift can only take place when there is a state of bilingual-ism as, clearly, no community can afford to abandon its language and become mute;
- in order for the speakers of one language to be attracted to another, there must be significant differences of prestige and status between the two languages (hence the term 'marked');
- the rate of language shift depends to a large degree on the amount of pressure (or attraction) from the dominant language on the one hand, and the degree of resistance from the minority language on the other.

The model can be applied synchronically by categorising a set of lan-guages according to their degree of language shift, or diachronically by looking at how the language shift process evolves over time or how the different age groups shift progressively to another language. The model postulates five phases that a language goes through on its way to extinction as its speakers shift progressively to the other language. These phases, which are described below, should be seen as arbitrary points in a continuum from one end of the process to the other.

Phase one: Relative monolingualism

The phase of relative monolingualism involves a situation in which the speakers of a language (referred to as L_1) are relatively monolingual. They may be in casual contact with other languages and some speakers may be bilingual, but the bulk of the speakers remain monolingual and use their language in all or most domains. The majority of the speakers are rural, conservative and not much exposed to education, urban life, migration or inter-ethnic activity. Many of the major languages or those spoken in remote or isolated areas would fall into this category.

Phase two: Bilingualism with L_1 predominance

This is a situation in which a dominant or more prestigious language, denoted by L_2, encroaches on L_1. Usually, L_2 is used as a lingua franca or second language in the secondary domains. A diglossic situation arises in which L_2 is used in the higher (H) public functions or for wider communication, such as inter-ethnic interaction, trade and local administration, while L_1 remains the language used in most village communication, intraethnic interaction and family life. It assumes the lower status (L). At this stage, L_1 is the more frequently used language as it is the medium used in most domains. Hence, it is the *primary medium* (Whiteley, 1971), while L_2 is the *secondary medium* as it is used only in specific situations. Thus, each language has its own defined domains of use. Instances of code-switching, interference and borrowing from L_2 are minimal at this stage. This is the situation that prevails when a language is in contact with a dominant language but is only using it for wider communication. Many of the relatively safe languages are in this phase.

Phase three: Bilingualism with L_2 predominance

The stage of bilingualism with L_2 predominance is reached when L_2 becomes the primary language. This happens because the L_1/L_2 relationship is asymmetrical, that is, one of unequal partners, and is therefore unstable. Due to the great prestige and more extensive use elsewhere of L_2, it is increasingly used in the other domains of L_1 until it assumes most of the domains that previously belonged to L_1. At this stage, L_2 becomes the most frequently used language and the form with which the speakers are more at ease. L_2 is now used even in village activities and some family interactions, while L_1 is restricted mostly to family and cultural activities. In this case, L_2 has become the primary medium and L_1 the secondary medium.

At this stage, we expect to see extensive code-switching and borrowing from L_2 when members of the community speak L_1. As observed by Myers-Scotton (1992) and Smieja (2000), code-switching to a massive extent is a sign that a language shift is imminent. A good proportion of the African languages are in this category – particularly the relatively small ones and those heavily influenced by dominant languages – and therefore highly endangered.

Phase four: Restricted use of/competence in L_1

This is the stage in which the use and even the competence in L_1 have become highly restricted. Such a stage is reached when the functions of L_1 are so reduced that people use L_1 forms only in specific situations, such as initiation ceremonies, rituals or folkloric performances. Such communities have lost the ability to use L_1 in its original form and, by implication, their stylistic competence in the language. In most cases they will not have learnt it properly, and so their structural competence is also greatly reduced. Only a few old men, and especially women, might still be familiar with the linguistic forms as originally used. Members of the community, however, might nevertheless assume that the language remains vibrant as part of their ethnic identity.

At this stage the language, which would now be considered as dying, has suffered not only a reduction in its stylistic expression but also significant simplification of its phonological system (Dressler, 1972) and heavy contraction in its morphology (Dimmendaal, 1998). Moreover, all the irregular forms tend to be regularised and simplified. Syntactic rules are reduced or made more general. The lexicon is also heavily reduced and may suffer many intrusions from L_2 (Williamson, 2003). This stage has been referred to elsewhere as *pidginisation* (Dimmendaal, 1989) or *creolisation* (Thomason & Kaufman, 1988). There seems to be a clear correspondence between the pidginisation process that affects languages in this category and the process of cultural erosion. Usually autonymic (personal names) and ethnonymic (ethnic name) forms are the last to be abandoned, except where the speakers develop some stigma about their identity, as has happened with many Khoesan communities in southern Africa.

Phase five: L_1 as a substratum

The predominance of L_2 may become so great that it replaces L_1 completely. This is the stage at which L_1 can be described as dead as it is no longer used in the community. However, the community may have kept its ethnonym and some of its traditions. Some of the linguistic characteristics of L_1 often remain as residual features in L_2. Such phenomena, known as *substratum features*, may involve prosodic, phonetic, phonological, semantic or lexical elements. A typical example is the clicks that are abundant in the Nguni and Sotho languages of southern Africa and which are remnants of extinct Khoesan languages. In some cases L_1 may disappear without leaving any linguistic traces.

Concluding remarks

Unfortunately, due to the often contradictory information, it is not always possible to be certain at what stage a language is on the continuum. It is particularly difficult to decide between phases four and five as it is not easy to ascertain whether the members of a given language group have disappeared altogether. Even if some are still alive, it is difficult to know to what extent a language is still being used. One good example is the case of Aasax in northern Tanzania, which was reported by Winter (1976) and Ehret (1980) to be extinct after the last speaker was presumed to have died of old age in 1976. However, Derek Nurse, as reported in Sommer (1992), found several Aasax speakers still alive in the 1980s.

According to the marked bilingualism model, there are two types of language contact situation: horizontal, termed *coordinate language contact*; and vertical, termed *superordinate language contact* (Batibo, 2003b). Coordinate language contact usually involves two languages of the same status such that neither language is able to dominate the other. The speakers of the two languages may learn each other's language mainly to interact and are not attracted to shifting. Thus, they can be bilingual without abandoning their language. This situation is referred to as *unmarked bilingualism*.

In contrast, superordinate language contact refers to the situation in which two languages with significantly different status and prestige come into contact. A vertical relationship results, with the more powerful language on top, giving rise to a diglossic structure. In most cases, L_1 will be overpowered by L_2, gradually giving way until language shift takes place. Where bilingualism offers the speakers of L_1 the potential for promotion in both the interactions open to them and their status or prestige, it is referred to as *marked bilingualism*.

Relevance of the Two Models to the African Situation
Introduction

As we have seen, the two models – the Gaelic–Arvanitika model and the marked bilingualism model – are complementary in that both capture the phenomena of language shift and death. The former focuses on the causes and effects of language domination, while the latter focuses on the processes involved from the time a language is dominated to the time it becomes extinct and is replaced by another. Both models have been used in several recent descriptions by other scholars of specific language situations (see, for example, Mekacha, 1993; Rubanza, 1994; Smieja, 2003).

The relevance of the two models to the African situation stems from the fact that they capture the three aspects of language shift that are common in the continent – the causes that trigger the phenomenon, the effects which follow, and the processes involved in language shift and death. These aspects will be highlighted below.

Common causes of language shift and death in Africa

As mentioned in Chapter 4, the main cause of language endangerment – and by implication language shift and death – is the pressure that the weaker languages experience from more powerful or prestigious languages. This pressure may be caused by demographic superiority, socio-economic attractions, political predominance or cultural forces.

Demographic pressure results when a language with a large number of speakers comes in contact with a language with fewer speakers. The usual tendency is for the minority speakers to want to identify themselves with the majority language speakers. This is happening with many of the major dominant languages like Hausa in West Africa, Kiswahili in East Africa and Setswana in southern Africa, which have attracted speakers of smaller languages largely because of their demographic might.

Socio-economic pressure arises when a language associated with socio-economic opportunities comes into contact with a language with little or no socio-economic power. Usually, national or regional lingua francas that are used as inter-ethnic languages for trade, education, administration, mass media or urban communication tend to attract speakers from other more localised languages. Again, the larger and more economically and socially privileged languages have extended their power over the socio-economically weaker languages.

Political pressure results when a language associated with power or political influence comes in contact with a language which has no such influence. Usually, the speakers of the weaker language will want to identify themselves with the more powerful language. An example is Setswana in Botswana, whose traditional chiefs rule over other groups and are responsible for the distribution of land and the administration of customary law. This has created a situation of dependence of the weaker groups on Setswana as the language of power. Thus, many speakers of Shiyeyi,

Chikuhane, Sebirwa, Setswapong, Shua, Tshwa, Kua and others are in the process of shifting to Setswana.

Cultural pressure comes about when a language with certain cultural forces, such as those associated with a religion or unique traditions, comes into contact with another language. The most common cases in Africa are the influence of languages like Arabic and to a lesser extent Kiswahili and Hausa, which are associated with Islam. Another example is Lingala, which has attracted many second-language speakers because of its association with music.

Apart from the above sources of pressure, there are other circumstances that have favoured the spread of the powerful or privileged languages by bringing them into contact or causing them to overlap with less powerful or privileged ones. These circumstances can be categorised as geo-demographic, socio-economic, political and sociolinguistic.

First, the geo-demographic circumstances comprise a number of geographical and demographic factors. These include the high concentration of languages in certain areas, which gives rise to many cases of contact, overlap, competition and conflict; imbalance in the sizes of languages, causing some languages to dominate the others; and the isolation of scattered groups, which may be 'swallowed up' by the larger groups and their languages.

Second, the socio-economic circumstances comprise economic and social factors such as migration into other communities, causing economic dependence; inter-marriages between groups, which favours the use of a common lingua franca; the rapid urbanisation and growth of commercial centres, which favour the use of the widely used languages; and less remunerative socio-economic activities such as pastoralism, agriculture, fishing, hunting, gathering and bee-keeping, which can lead to dependence

Third, the political circumstances consist of factors like the promotion of certain languages to a new status, such as national or official language, thus conferring power and privilege on such languages; the domination of one language by another due to the belligerent or aggressive nature of the stronger group (Childs, 2003); or the feelings of inferiority of the weaker group (Batibo, 1998). Some groups have also been described as being too open to strangers, meaning that they welcome interaction and intermingling with other groups and may as a result adopt their languages or culture (Childs, 2003).

Last, the sociolinguistic circumstances include usage-related factors such as inequality in the public use of the languages and the complex patterns of language use, which favour certain languages but may cause others to become redundant or marginalised.

Effects of the pressure

A weaker language (L_1) experiences many effects due to the pressure from the stronger language (L_2). The effects may include the following:

- assumption by L_2 of the higher status in the pattern of language use, so that it is used in inter-ethnic domains such as trade, administration and wider communication;
- diminishing domains of use of L_1 in favour of L_2, to the extent that L_1 is retained mainly for cultural expression and secret ritual;
- the development of negative attitudes towards L_1 since it is seen as a language of no socio-economic value;
- progressive imperfection in the learning of L_1, with eventual ceasing of transmission of L_1 as children acquire only L_2;
- progressive reduction in the stylistic variation and structural complexity of L_1 as it becomes simplified or pidginised;
- massive language interference, code-switching and borrowing from L_2 as L_1 becomes totally 'invaded' by the former;
- progressive lexical impoverishment of L_1 as children fail to acquire the full range of vocabulary (Williamson, 2003).

The above effects need not all occur at the same time, and some will be more prominent than others. Moreover, the linguistic reduction of L_1 will tend to coincide with cultural reduction as well.

The process dimension

Where the pressure from L_2 is greater than the degree of resistance from L_1, it must be concluded that the process of language shift is in progress. The lower the resistance, the more rapid the process will be. Thus the small, weak languages are usually the most vulnerable. As described in the marked bilingualism model, many African languages are progressively succumbing to the pressures of L_2 and are therefore gradually giving up their domains until they reach a stage where they become redundant as L_2 takes over all the domains of language use. It is only when there is enough resistance from L_1 that a somewhat diglossic situation can be maintained.

When is a Language Extinct?

Usually, a language is described as extinct when it is no longer used. As described above, language death may result in many ways. There are two main possibilities: a *sudden death*; or a *gradual death*. Language death is described as sudden if the extinction occurs over a relatively short time. The most common cause would be genocide, which was the case during the European conquest of Australia and the Americas, where many language communities were wiped out; or the fate of the Khoesan groups in southern Africa when the Bantu communities moved in more than 1000 years ago. Another cause of sudden death may be an epidemic disease which wipes out a whole community, as in the case of the Mastuthunira community in Australia, which perished over a short period due to a series of epidemic diseases (Bobaljik *et al.*, 1996). Yet another type is when a whole community decides to abandon a language, usually as an integrative strategy, as was described by Gal (1979) in the case of the immigrants from Hungary into Austria. Language abandonment has been described elsewhere as 'suicide language death' (Dorian, 1977).

The most common form of language death, as is currently experienced in Africa, is the gradual type in which a language becomes extinct due to a gradual shift of its speakers to another language. This may involve a progressive increase in the domains accorded to the dominant language, with eventual *absorption* of the community into the dominant one; or the use of a certain amount of pressure, which may result in language *suffocation*. Gradual language death may also lead to structural decay, in which a language becomes no longer functional due either to *erosion*, that is, the over-simplification of its forms, or *contraction*, that is, the reduction of its rules to a non-functional level.

The processes of gradual and sudden language death according to the marked bilingualism model are shown schematically in Figure 4.

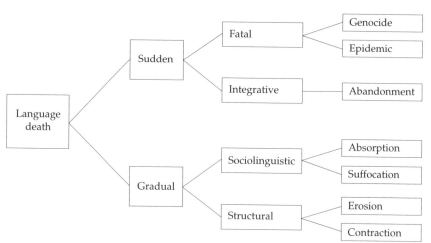

Figure 4 The various circumstances of language death according to the marked bilingualism model (Batibo, 1992, 1997)

Although one may say that a language is presumed to be extinct when it is no longer spoken or used, the problem of exactly *when* a language dies is much more complex. Does a language become extinct when the last speaker dies? Or when the speakers, although they may still know the language, no longer use it in normal communication? Or when its structural forms are no longer available for use although they still exist in a simplified or residual form? Or does it occur when it is no longer spoken but can still be written, such as Latin or classical Greek? What if there remain some speakers of a different dialect or variety? These questions are highly pertinent in the African situation as there are often controversies as to whether a given language has really become extinct or not.

The Role of Attitudes to Language

An attitude could be defined as a feeling, reaction or emotional disposition towards an idea, concept or phenomenon. According to Baker (1992: 12), an attitude has three components: the cognitive, involving thought and beliefs; the affective, concerned with feelings and emotions; and the connotative, referring to a readiness to act. Where languages are concerned, all three components are involved as an attitude to a language could be described as consisting of a mental disposition, an emotional feeling and a reaction. Such feelings could be positive, negative or indifferent.

Usually, monolingual speakers have only one attitude towards their language because they have no other languages to compare it with. Such an attitude would normally be positive as they see their language as a central means for communication, socialisation and ethnic identity. However, where speakers become bilingual, there is a tendency to develop different attitudes to each of the languages used. These attitudes, whether positive or negative, will normally depend on the degree of symbolic or socio-economic value manifested by each language. Usually, L_1 will have symbolic value as a mother tongue and language of ethnic identity, and L_2, as the second language, may have socio-economic value as the inter-ethnic language and may be associated with trade, education, employment or administration. The situation becomes more complex in a triglossic situation in which three languages are used, not only for different functions but also with different symbolic and socio-economic values. Generally, L_1, as the mother tongue, will have symbolic value as the language of cultural and ethnic identity but will usually have little or no socio-economic prestige; L_2, as the inter-ethnic language, will have considerable socio-economic prestige; while L_3, as the official or national language (usually the ex-colonial language), will enjoy the highest social status and socio-economic

Table 12 Language attitudes among the Khoesan speakers of northeastern Botswana

Item	Positive response (%)				
	L_1	L_1 & L_2	L_2	L_2 & L_3	L_3
Language that parents would like children to speak at home	6.9	0.0	79.3	13.8	0.0
Language that parents would like to be used as medium at school	0.0	6.5	58.1	32.3	3.2
Language that should be used in their community	16.6	26.7	56.7	0.0	0.0
Origin of names given to children	19.2	19.6	51.6	6.4	3.3
Speakers should be known under which identity	71.4	0.0	28.6	0.0	0.0

Source: After Batibo (1998: 268). L_1, mother tongue; L_2, national language (Setswana); L_3, ex-colonial language (English)

prestige. Language attitudes usually, although not always, follow the socio-economic hierarchy. The more prestigious a language, the more positive the speakers' attitude is towards it, and the less prestigious a language, the more negative the attitudes are.

Most parents wish their children to have proficiency in the ex-colonial language to improve their chances of social promotion and economic advancement, even at the expense of their mother tongue. However, in many African communities, as rightly observed by Adegbija (1994), the ex-colonial language is restricted to a small proportion of the elite. The only prestigious language would therefore be the prominent lingua franca, L_2. In many cases, therefore, parents want their children to be proficient in L_2 instead of L_1. Such an attitude contributes greatly to the language shift process. Table 12 presents some results of a case study of two Khoesan communities in northeastern Botswana who have developed positive attitudes or a preference for Setswana, the national language and lingua franca (L_2), at the expense of their own mother tongues, Shua and |Xaise (L_1).

At the same time, English, the ex-colonial language (L_3), does not seem to play as much of a role as Setswana in the Khoesan communities, as demonstrated by the low figures in the last column.

What is significant in Table 12 is that although the two communities want their children to be more proficient in Setswana, to use it as a medium in school and to give the children Setswana names, they want to preserve their ethnic name. As has been shown elsewhere (Chebanne & Nthapelelang, 2000), ethnonymic identity is usually the last feature of identity to be lost in a community after both language and culture have been abandoned.

The Effect of Language Promotion on Minority Languages

In a number of African countries some of the major languages have been promoted to the role of a national and/or official language, examples being Setswana in Botswana, Kiswahili in Kenya and Tanzania, Amharic in Ethiopia, Chichewa in Malawi (during President Kamuzu Banda's regime) and Somali in Somalia. Where such status promotion has been associated with an actual expanded use of these languages in public functions, not only have their social status and prestige increased but their utilisation value has also been augmented. This, in turn, has given such languages more weight relative to the minority languages, making the latter more vulnerable. In Tanzania, for example, the elevation of Kiswahili to national and official levels in the 1960s increased its predominance and influence over the other languages, and as a result it expanded enormously throughout the country. Batibo (1992) and Mkude (2001) have described how the process of language shift due to Kiswahili domination has accelerated. As correctly observed by Bernd Heine (pers. comm.), the main threat to the African languages at present is not the ex-colonial languages (confined as they are mainly to a small number of the elite) or the minor areally dominant languages (as they are not as powerful), but rather the nationally and major areally dominant languages as these are often promoted and supported by the state. As shown by Mekacha (1993) for the case of Kiswahili (see Table 13), such languages are rapidly replacing both the ex-colonial and the minority languages.

Summary and Conclusions

Language shift results when speakers of a given language abandon their language, either willingly or under pressure, in favour of another, which then takes over as their means of communication and socialisation. Language death results when a language becomes extinct, that is, when it

Table 13 The upward and downward expansion of Kiswahili due to its national predominance in Tanzania

Type of function	English	Kiswahili	Minority language
State	Yes	Yes	No
Inter-ethnic	No	Yes	No
Intra-ethnic	No	Yes	Yes

Source: Based on Mekacha (1993: 10)

is no longer used as a means of communication or socialisation. There are two major theoretical perspectives on language shift and death, one causality-based and the other process-based. A typical model that uses the first approach is the Gaelic–Arvanitika model (GAM), which is based on three aspects of language death. These are the *external setting*, which considers the extra-linguistic causes of language death; *speech behaviour*, which comprises the change in attitudes and language behaviour that follow; and the *structural consequences*, which involves all the linguistic changes that take place.

A model of the second type – that using the process-based approach – is the marked bilingualism model (MBM), which looks at the various stages a language community goes through in shifting from its original language, L_1, to the new language, L_2. The process usually begins with a relatively monolingual situation; then a dominant language encroaches, taking over the upper domains of language use as a secondary medium. However, because of the privileged position of L_2, it gradually takes over most of the domains of language use and therefore becomes the primary medium. In the end, L_2 becomes the sole medium of the community as L_1 is made redundant.

Both models are relevant to the African situation as they capture the three important aspects of language shift and death, namely the causes, the effects and the processes involved. The main cause of language shift is the pressure that a dominant language exerts on a weaker language. The pressure may be demographic, socio-economic, political or cultural. Usually, a language is described as extinct when it is no longer used. Language death may be sudden, as in genocide, epidemics and abandonment, or gradual, as when there is progressive pressure from the dominant language. One major question is when a language can be presumed to be extinct, as it may not be spoken but some former speakers are still living, or it remains in use as a written language.

The language attitudes of the speakers play an important role as strong resistance to language shift is usually only possible if speakers have a positive attitude to their language and hold it in high regard. Where a language is felt to have little socio-economic value or social prestige, speakers may put up little resistance and are more inclined to abandon it in favour of one with greater prestige. Thus, in Africa the most vulnerable languages are the small, marginalised ones as they lack demographic power, the economic attractions or the social status of dominant languages. The speakers easily cultivate negative attitudes towards them and encourage their children to learn the more prestigious languages instead.

Chapter 7

Language Maintenance in Africa

Language Shift and Maintenance in Contact Situations

Language maintenance is a situation in which a language maintains its vitality, even under pressure. It implies, therefore, that the degree of resistance is strong enough to contain any pressure that may be coming from a dominant language. In a situation of language maintenance, the domains of language L_1 remain largely the same and transmission of the language to the children is active and as perfect as possible. Moreover, the number of speakers remains relatively stable and they maintain a strong allegiance to their language. Language maintenance usually applies to a relatively monolingual situation. However, it may take place in a stable diglossic situation, in which the functions of L_1 and L_2 are well defined and remain unchanged. As mentioned in Chapter 2, the stability of a diglossic or triglossic situation is often difficult to maintain because of the inequality in the status of the languages concerned, which means that speakers of L_1 (the low-status language) must resist encroachment by L_2 (the high-status language) if the situation is to remain undisturbed.

When two languages are in contact, their relationship is either *coordinate* (that is, the speakers learn each other's languages on equal grounds so as to interact with each other) or *superordinate* (the speakers of the weaker language learn the speech of the stronger or more prestigious language for wider communication or socio-economic gains). In the first case, the model of language contact involves a horizontal contact relationship that gives rise to bilingualism. This model is shown in Figure 5.

In this type of contact, language maintenance will normally prevail as the speakers of L_1 will only use L_2 when communicating and interacting with the other ethnic group. Since L_2, as a mainly intra-ethnic language, will have no conspicuous prestige, status or socio-economic attraction in relation to L_1, there will be no motivation for L_1 speakers to shift to L_2. The scenario presented above is, in a way, theoretical, as in reality one of the two languages will have an edge over the other in terms of numbers,

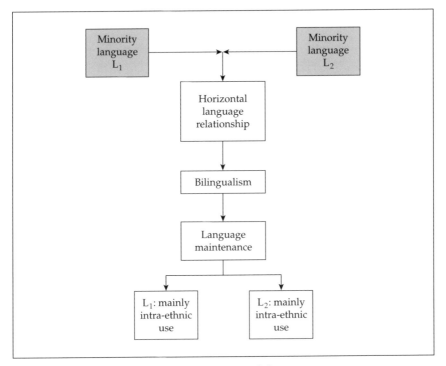

Figure 5 Coordinate language contact model

prestige, status or dynamism of the speakers. But as long as this inequality is not significant, there will be no strong need for L_1 speakers to abandon their language in favour of L_2. They will only use L_2 as an interactive medium. Thus, the situation will be one of *unmarked bilingualism*. Given that the majority of languages in Africa are minority languages, this type of language contact is presumed to be the most common.

When there is superordinate language contact, L_2 tends to dominate L_1 as it is more prestigious, more powerful, more socio-economically attractive or more widely used. In this case, a diglossic situation may arise in which L_2 is used by L_1 speakers in the higher or more public domains, while L_1 remains the medium of intra-ethnic and family communication as well as of cultural expression. Depending on the degree of resistance of L_1, the diglossic balance between L_1 and L_2 may be stable, resulting in the maintenance of L_1, or unstable, resulting in the progressive reduction of the domains of L_1, as described in the marked bilingualism model in Chapter 6. The model for the second scenario is shown in Figure 6.

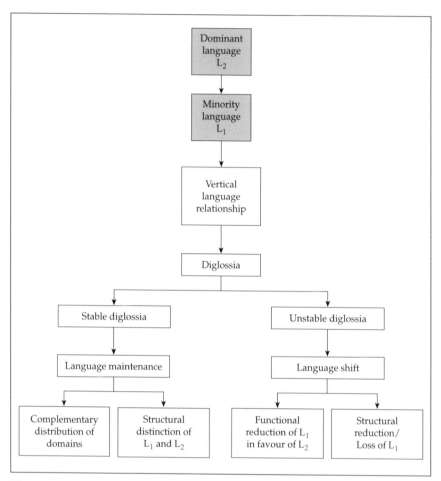

Figure 6 Superordinate language contact model

With superordinate language contact, language shift is likely to take place as the speakers of L_1 will use L_2 for both interaction and status promotion, and therefore will gradually want to shift to the more prestigious language. If L_1 is to be maintained, speakers must find some value in the language so that continuing to transmit it to the younger generations is felt to be worthwhile. As discussed above, the most important factor in diglossic stability is the language attitude towards L_1, which is usually moulded by perception of socio-economic or cultural factors in respect of L_1. Some languages are able to sustain themselves better than others.

Auburger's Theory of Language Maintenance

A number of theories have been proposed to suggest how a diglossic situation may be maintained. One of these has been advanced by Leopold Auburger under the name of the 'proficiency resistance model' (Auburger, 1990: 180ff). According to this model, there are at least five factors that help to sustain proficiency in a minority language where the speakers are confronted by a dominant language. These factors can be summarised as:

- a strict diglossic use of the minority and dominant languages;
- a written mode of the minority language to enhance the oral mode;
- an emotional attachment to the minority language, resulting in sensitivity to correctness and purity in its use;
- a successful process of learning the minority language with a sustainable level proficiency;
- a process of reinforcement of the community by the settling of other speakers of the language from the main source of origin.

Although the provisions of this model may be difficult to find in many African languages, it proved possible in a study carried out by Batibo and Tsonope in 1999 on Nama speakers of Matlhatlaganyane Ward of Tsabong in southwest Botswana. This Nama community of only about 300 speakers in the middle of a mainly Setswana- and Shekgalagadi-speaking area had managed to maintain the vitality of their language. It turned out from the study (Batibo & Tsonope, 2000: 48–54) that the situation of the speakers corresponded well with the factors described in Auburger's model.

First, there was a reasonably stable diglossic use of the minority and majority languages, in that the minority language (Nama) was used in the family and in intra-ethnic communication, while the majority language (Setswana) was used in inter-ethnic interaction. As Table 14 shows, the higher figures for Nama were in the family and intra-ethnic domains, while the higher figures for Setswana were in the inter-ethnic domains.

Second, the Matlhatlaganyane Nama people had a tradition of a written mode. Several adults and old people could read and, to a lesser extent, write in Nama. This tradition bestowed on the language a symbolic status and great esteem, hence reinforcing its active use.

Third, there was a substantial emotional attachment to Nama, particularly among the older generation. Furthermore, a traditional correctness and purity of usage were strictly observed. This ensured that transmission of the language to children remained as perfect as possible.

Fourth, there was a regular process of reinforcement, not by in-migration (settling of new speakers) but by constant visits by relatives from Namibia, where the majority of the Nama people live.

Table 14 Patterns of language use (% of respondents) in Matlhatlaganyane Ward of Tsabong village, southwest Botswana

Language	In the family	Intra-ethnic communication	Inter-ethnic communication
Nama	59.0	51.3	11.6
Nama/Setswana	23.1	33.3	10.3
Setswana	7.7	10.3	75.7
Shekgalagari	2.6	0.0	2.6
Nama/Shekgalagari	26.0	0.0	0.0
Nama/Setswana/ Afrikaans	26.0	2.6	0.0
Nama/Setswana/ English	0.0	2.6	0.0

Source: After Batibo & Tsonope (2000: 49). Totals do not necessarily add to 100% because of the many overlaps in the information provided by the respondents

Thus, although the population of Nama speakers in Tsabong was only 300 in a large village of over 15,000 people, they had managed to maintain their language and keep it highly vibrant.

Cases like that of Nama in Matlhatlaganyane Ward of Tsabong are not common in Africa as most minority languages do not find themselves in such favourable conditions. In most instances, therefore, the question would not be one of language maintenance but the rate at which a language shift is taking place.

Proposed Guidelines for Language Maintenance

Some scholars have attempted to come up with guidelines on language maintenance. One of these scholars is Blench (1998). His set of guidelines can be listed as follows:

- absence of an adjacent culturally dominant group;
- endogamous marriage practices;
- maintenance of traditional religion/cultural pride;
- existence of an orthography;
- government oppression and neglect;
- remoteness;
- access to media;
- demographic expansion.

The above factors could be regarded as favourable circumstances for language maintenance insofar as they involve relative isolation, non-interference by another group, strong attachment to a culture or religion, language codification, enhancement of the language through the media and increasing numbers. These circumstances are favourable not only in language maintenance but also in language revival where there has been a trend towards decline. However, what is most unusual in the list is the suggestion that there should be government oppression and neglect. This is presumably meant to emphasise the fact that high sensitivity and extreme involvement are required of the speakers.

In Africa, language maintenance still prevails where the speakers are either demographically important or strongly attached to their culture and traditions. Blench (1998: 200) gives an example of two Chadic languages, Lopa and Laru of Lake Kainji, which in spite of the small numbers of those who speak them have managed to maintain themselves. Likewise Boni, a Cushitic language spoken in eastern Africa, has managed, to some degree, to maintain itself in spite of the small number of speakers (Tosco, 1992). In both cases the speakers are highly attached to their languages for reasons of both culture and self-identity. Languages such as Coptic and Ge'ez have maintained themselves, at least in a written form, mainly because of their use as languages of religious expression; while others, like Fulani, have managed to keep their vitality due to the traditional high social status of the speakers as pastoralists.

Language maintenance is usually reinforced by a tradition of a written form as this tends to raise its social and symbolic status. In Africa there are many languages which have managed to maintain themselves to varying degrees depending on size, vitality, social status, levels of public use and speakers' attitudes. However, in the final analysis one should remember that all languages in the world are part of a food chain in which, at the one end, there is English, the super-international language that dominates all the languages of the world, and, at the other end, there are the weakest languages. Every language except English is under some form of pressure. This all means that, apart from English, the maintenance of the world's languages is a relative matter. Some languages are able to sustain themselves better than others.

The Role of Attitudes in Language Maintenance

The role of attitudes in language maintenance, just as in language shift, has been recognised by a number of scholars (Adegbija, 1996; Batibo, 1992, 1997, 1998, 2003a; Chebanne & Nthapelelang, 2000; Smieja, 1999, 2003). This is because the speakers of a language hold the key to the continuation of abandonment of their language, the intertransmission or distransmission of the language to their children and the expansion or reduction of the domains in which it is used. However, the speakers' attitudes depend heavily on the status and prestige of their language (Smieja, 2003: 63). Such prestige results from their perception of its symbolic or utilitarian value. The social esteem in which a language is held is often a function of favourable government policies, historical legacy, extensive domains of use, a well-codified form of the language, substantial documentation or cultural prestige.

The question of attitude also depends on the way the speakers view their language in relation to other languages. Where there is low self-esteem by the speakers or negative evaluation by others, the former may not maintain their language in its full vitality. Overall, language maintenance is difficult where there is a substantial influence from a dominant language.

The Role of National Language Policies

National language policies may help to preserve or maintain a language if they support some practical or utilitarian use of a language. However, in order for a national language policy to be useful in language maintenance, it must be implemented. Thus, although the Namibian government has instituted a supportive language policy that promotes all indigenous languages to national language status, the policy has not materially affected the maintenance of these languages as it is seen as merely symbolic. No measures have been implemented to give such languages the utilitarian value that might be expected. English and Afrikaans remain the languages of social and economic promotion in Namibia.

Where national policies visibly support the codification of languages and their active use in public and socio-economic spheres, the utilitarian value of those languages has increased, giving them higher social status and prestige. The speakers have, in turn, become active users of the languages. One such example is Malawi, where the government of President Bakili Muluzi decided to promote not only the traditionally favoured language, Chichewa (Chinyanja), but also the other major languages, such as Chitumbuka and Chiyao. The latter were rigorously codified, documented and introduced into the education system. This move has enhanced their social status and prestige, and the speakers have become very enthusiastic to see their languages developed and used in some of the key areas of public life, such as education and the mass media.

Unfortunately, in most African countries there are no explicit language policies that favour active public use of the indigenous languages. Even where such policies exist, as in the case of South Africa and Namibia, the implementation part has often lagged behind.

Language Survival and Revival

The world has seen a number of cases where languages were on the verge of extinction but managed to survive and even revitalise themselves. The most typical example is that of Modern Hebrew, which reached the point of near extinction in the 19th century. The language was successfully revitalised during the creation of the Jewish state of Israel and has now become the official and national language of modern Israel (Fishman, 1991: 291). The revival of Modern Hebrew was greatly facilitated by its coincidence with the creation of an independent nation in which the language is used not only as a means of communication but also as a symbol of nationalism, solidarity and national identity.

Other instances of language revival that have had varying degrees of success include French in Quebec, Catalan in Spain, Yiddish in New York and Los Angeles, Navajo in Arizona, USA, and Maori in New Zealand. However, although these have generally been described as success stories (Bobaljik *et al.*, 1996), one needs to remark that the level of revitalisation in each case has been relative. The position of languages such as Yiddish and Maori is still unclear despite some intense efforts at revitalisation, and Navajo and Copper Island Aleut are not completely safe. In a number of cases attempts to revitalise languages have not borne fruit. One typical example where revival efforts have failed is the case of Irish in Ireland (Carnie, 1996: 99; Fishman, 1991: 122; Slomanson, 1996: 115).

In general, success in the revival of a threatened language depends on a number of factors. A language can only be revived if it has not yet reached a point of no return. Fishman (1991) devised a vitality scale, which he named GILD (graded intergenerational disruption scale). According to this scale, the level of vitality of a language can be measured in terms of the age group in which a language is still spoken. If a language is still spoken by those of child-bearing age (say, 20–45), the chances of the parents passing the language on to the children is high as long as the parents are encouraged or given incentives to do so. But if the language is only spoken by those of non-child-bearing age (60 and above), the chances would be that even if encouraged or given an incentive, parents would not be able to pass it on to their children as only the old people speak the language. This is what is currently happening among the Nama-speaking Ovaherero of the Tsabong area of southwest Botswana, where the Ovaherero are unable to transmit their ethnic language, Otjiherero, to the younger generation in spite of their great desire to do so because all the child-bearing Ovaherero speak only Nama or Setswana (Batibo, 2003a).

Language revival is often facilitated by a lessening of the dominance of the language that is causing the language shift process. This lessening could be brought about either by emigration of the weaker group to a more remote area or by seclusion of the group, as in the cases of the Navajo and the Basque. An interesting case is that of Copper Island Aleut in eastern Russia, where the language has managed to revitalise itself in recent years mainly because of the lessened influence of the Russian language following the fall of the Soviet Union (Vakhtin, 1998: 317). On the other hand, one reason why the efforts to revitalise the Irish language have not succeeded is the continued presence of the dominant language, English, which has continued to attract allegiance because of its internationality and socio-economic benefits.

Language revival efforts are likely to bear fruit if they are reinforced by in-migration as this tends to increase the number of speakers and increase their self-confidence. An example is Catalan in Spain, which was strongly reinforced by the in-migration of people who spoke the language. Again, one of the contributing factors to the failure of the revival of Irish has been the emigration of a good number of Irish speakers to America, as this tended to reduce the number of speakers and lessen confidence among those who remained in preserving their language and culture (Carnie, 1996: 99).

Language revival may be made more effective by the introduction of a well-planned and aggressive set of measures whereby not only are the speakers involved and take the leading role but the national institutions are also made to play a supportive role. This is what happened in the case of the Maori language in New Zealand, where the Maori Social and Economic Advancement Act of 1945 set the ball rolling. The result was a high level of motivation and involvement by Maori speakers as well as by the relevant institutions in support of the national and local measures taken to revitalise Maori language and culture.

Finally, as pointed out by Dorian (1998: 3), language loss or gain is directly linked to the high or low social prestige of the speakers. The lower their social prestige, the more likely a language is to be lost, and the higher their social prestige, the more likely it is that the language will gain ground. Language revival is therefore possible only where the social prestige of the speakers within the language community has been elevated in some way. Such elevation in social prestige could be brought about through improved education, economic independence, ownership of property such as land, political autonomy or self-determination. On the other hand, a language may be revitalised even where there has been no significant elevation of the social status of the speakers, as has happened with Kishaba, a sub-dialect of Kiswahili spoken in Shaba Province in the southeast of the Democratic Republic of Congo. This variety has managed to prevail over the standard form and even become more vibrant because of several local socio-cultural factors, such as solidarity and strong cultural attachment, that have motivated the speakers' active use of the language (Kapanga, 1998).

Very little has been documented on the processes of language revival or revitalisation in an African context. There are instances of emancipation where groups have demanded to have more rights in their communities. Such manifestations are often linked to a desire for freedom in the use or promotion of an indigenous language and culture. This type of cultural awareness has also been instrumental in the creation of positive attitudes towards one's language and the will to preserve and actively use it.

In a number of countries, such as Tanzania, Malawi, Ethiopia and Botswana, there has been a wave of ethnic awareness, and even conflict, which has reached a point where it poses a considerable challenge to the nationalistic ideal of creating a unified nation-state. Such ethnic insurgencies are motivated not only by the wish to preserve indigenous languages and cultures but also to sensitise the authorities to recognise and appreciate the linguistic and cultural diversity of the respective countries. Such moves may, to a certain extent, serve to reinforce language survival and revitalisation. However, language revival can only succeed where the efforts of the speakers and the support of national institutions become more powerful than the original circumstances which were causing the process of language shift.

UNESCO has begun a new programme to safeguard the endangered languages of the world under its special unit, the Intangible Heritage Section. In collaboration with language specialists and other concerned members of the international community, it has formulated a set of guidelines for the assessment of language vitality, which it has published in a document entitled 'Language Vitality and Endangerment' (UNESCO, 2003b). In addition, a series of action-plan recommendations have been put forward that address the role of language communities, linguists, language advocates, non-governmental organisations (NGOs) and UNESCO itself. The main emphasis has been that all activities towards the revitalisation, maintenance or perpetuation of an endangered language should be undertaken in collaboration with the relevant communities.

A major question that has preoccupied UNESCO and its collaborators in matters of language revitalisation is what can be done to safeguard endangered languages. As an aid to the important task of making an appropriate assessment of the situation of a language that appears to be threatened,

UNESCO (2003a) has proposed nine major factors to gauge its vitality and state of endangerment. These factors are:

- *Intergenerational transmission* The more transmission there is from one generation to the next, the stronger the language is.
- *Absolute number of speakers* A small community is usually more vulnerable than a larger one when faced with disasters such as disease, warfare, natural catastrophes or merger with a larger group. However, a community with a strong sense of identity will be in a better position to maintain its language.
- *Proportion of speakers within the group* The number of speakers relative to the total population of a language group is a significant indicator of language vitality.
- *Loss of existing language domains* The more consistently and persistently the language is used, the stronger the language is. Thus, it is important to know the type and range of domains in which the language is used.
- *Response to new domains and media* The more actively the language is used in new domains, the stronger it is. This is because a language needs to be adaptable to any new conditions its speakers may encounter to allow its continued use.
- *Existence of materials for language educational literacy* The greater the variety of materials available in the language, and the more they are used in education, the stronger the language is. This is because a language is usually better maintained if education is conducted in the language with materials in oral, written and other forms.
- *Governmental and institutional language attitudes and policies* The more positive official attitudes and policies are towards the language of the community, the stronger the language is. Usually the language attitudes harboured by the dominant group or major neighbouring language groups towards the minority languages have a considerable impact on the maintenance or abandonment of those languages.
- *Community members' attitudes towards their own languages* The more positive their attitudes are and the more pride they take in their language, the stronger it is. In fact, the more value they attach to their traditions, the more likely the community is to maintain or promote its language.
- *Amount and quality of documentation* The more historical and contemporary materials there are on the language, the stronger it is.

According to UNESCO (2003b), a language is usually strong if it has comprehensive grammars and dictionaries, a good range of reading texts, a constant flow of publications, and abundant, annotated, high-quality audio and video recordings. Speakers of minority languages become more positive towards their language once they see an orthography and documents written in it.

Summary and Conclusions

In a situation where a language is being successfully maintained, the domains of L_1 will remain the same, the transmission of the language to the younger generation will be active and as perfect as possible, the number of speakers will remain relatively stable and the speakers will maintain a strong allegiance to their language. Although language maintenance is easier in a monolingual situation where the speakers have only one allegiance, it can also take place in bilingual or multilingual situations if there is enough stability in the use of the various domains for a stable diglossic or triglossic structure to prevail.

According to Auburger's (1990) proficiency resistance model, such stability can only result if there is a strict diglossic situation, a written mode of the minority language, strong emotional attachment by the speakers, a normal intertransmission of the language and regular reinforcement by in-migration. In more recent years a number of international organisations and non-governmental groups have shown concern over the global trend to language shift and death. Equally, some individual scholars have come up with guidelines for language maintenance and even revitalisation. These include intergenerational language transmission, maintenance of speaker numbers, stability of language domains, the ability to respond to new domains, preparation of educational materials, institutional support, positive speakers' attitudes and good documentation. Such guidelines, in a way, coincide with those presented in Auburger's model or in the guidelines proposed by scholars such as Blench (1998).

In Africa, there are many languages that have managed to maintain themselves to varying degrees, depending on size, vitality, social status, levels of public use and speakers' attitudes. Given the hierarchy of global language dominance, all world languages except English are under some degree of pressure from a language at a higher level. Speakers' attitudes towards their language are a key factor in language maintenance. This is because the speakers of a language hold the key to the continuation or abandonment in the use of their language, the intertransmission or distransmission of their language to their children and the expansion or reduction of its domains of use. On the other hand, speakers' attitudes depend to a very large extent on the status and prestige of their language.

Hence, national language policies are important as they determine the national role that a language is going to play, indirectly determining its utilitarian value.

Some languages that were on the verge of extinction have been saved by language revival actions. According to Sasse (1992: 21), language revitalisation can only be successful if there is removal of the social pressure exerted by the dominant group. This can be achieved by socio-political change, migration or gain of prestige by the affected language community. This would then give rise to a revitalised transmission of the language and an extension in its domains of use.

Unfortunately, in Africa the conditions for language revival hardly exist in view of the fact that the stronger languages continue to dominate the minority languages, language emigration is no longer a common practice and gains in the prestige of minority languages are not a common phenomenon. Only if there is a strong political will associated with a chain of activities such as the sensitisation of speakers, documentation of the minority languages, their introduction in school systems and promotion to wider public use will language revival succeed.

Chapter 8
Language Empowerment Measures

Processes of Language Empowerment

What has emerged so far in our discussion is that Africa is a plurilingual continent in which three categories of languages exist: the ex-colonial languages, the dominant indigenous languages and the minority languages. The first two categories are privileged in that they usually enjoy high social status and prestige, utilitarian functions and considerable socio-political power. People who belong to or have proficiency in these languages are the 'empowered' ones. In contrast, the languages in the third category, although in the majority in most countries, are often ignored, marginalised or accorded low status. As stated in Chapter 4, these languages suffer many disadvantages, which include a weak demographic position, low social status, lack of proper orthographies and documentation, limited public use, and often a history of socio-economic or political domination by a more powerful language group. As a result, the children of the minority language groups may have to learn through a different medium and may end up having problems in coping with the school environment as well as with their cognitive and affective development. Similarly, the adults are forced to use a second language when dealing with important issues that affect their lives. They may find it difficult to participate in national affairs or gain access to important information that concerns them. Hence, the people who speak these languages could be referred to as the 'powerless' (Bamgbose, 2000: 16).

In order to ensure that the speakers of the minority languages are not disadvantaged by their language situation, measures have to be taken to empower their languages. *Language empowerment* refers to the institution of a set of measures to raise the social status of a language as well as to make it more viable in handling public domains. According to Bamgbose (2000: 17), there are a number of measures that can be instituted to empower a language. These include a charter of linguistic human rights, appropriate legislation, language development, the adoption of second language norms, use of language in education, provision of incentives to users, and expansion of domains of use. Certainly African governments and policy-makers need first to be given the impetus to realise the importance of appropriate language policies involving the minority languages. Such an impetus could be given by, among others, the institution of true democracy, along with measures to ensure the participation of minority groups in national affairs and the right of all people to have access to education and information in the languages in which they are most proficient.

The measures to empower languages can be divided into the ideological and the technical. The ideological measures are those which concern the decision-makers. Each country's government and its associated institutions should come up with the following measures:

- explicit language policies that specify not only which should be the official or national language(s) but also which language should be used in which domain;
- the national language policy should take into account the plurilingual nature of a country and, therefore, as far as possible allocate roles to each language according to size, geographical location, vitality and level of development;
- the national language policy should take into consideration existing charters of linguistic human rights (although, as noted by Bamgbose (2000: 18), the content of such charters should be made use of in accordance with the realities prevailing in each country);
- the decision-makers should decide which variety or standard form of each language is to be used, such as which norms of English or French to adopt or which dialect of the main language should be regarded as the standard form, and so on.

Unfortunately, in spite of the 1986 Charter of the Organisation of African Unity (OAU, now African Union or AU), which encouraged African countries to have clear and explicit language policies, few have taken tangible steps to this end. The Charter advocated the use of African languages in all spheres. The same emphasis was made at the UNESCO-sponsored conference in Harare in 1997, which echoed the call for the empowerment of African languages. Countries such as Botswana, Tanzania, Kenya, Namibia and South Africa, which have relatively explicit language policies, appear to be the exceptions. Many of the other countries have remained silent on the question of language policy and only deal with language policy issues in a pragmatic manner. Others have decided to embrace the ex-colonial language as the only recognised official language, remaining silent on the indigenous languages. Yet another group of countries has recognised only the major languages and promoted them to national status. However, in all the above cases, no systematic mechanisms or schedules of implementation have been instituted for the minority languages, except in some restricted cases where these languages have been introduced as instructional media in lower primary education. As a result, in most countries the ruling elite has remained the empowered group as it uses an ex-colonial language that has been designated as the official language.

As regards the technical aspect of language empowerment, a language is made more capable through the process of technicisation, which refers to a set of measures taken to meet the various needs of the speakers, including those that involve public interaction. These measures will be discussed in the next section under 'Technical planning'.

Language Planning in Africa

Definition of language planning

A famous question, which was posed in the title of a book edited by Rubin & Jernudd (1971), is 'Can language be planned?' The whole idea of language planning was brought about by the thinking that language, as a resource, can be treated in economic terms, in much the same way as other resources in a nation's economy, where resources are planned for optimal use (Bamgbose, 1991: 30; Jernudd & Das Gupta, 1971: 195–6). Hence, language use can be subjected to cost–benefit analysis – that is, one asks what could be gained by choosing another language for a given purpose, or how the use of a language can be optimised so that it renders the best returns at the least cost. At a practical level, therefore, the questions to ask under language planning include: what does a nation gain or lose by promoting an indigenous language in some domains instead of using an ex-colonial language? Or, what does an individual gain or lose by using a mother tongue rather than a dominant language?

Although in today's world there is a correlation between the demand for a certain language, say English, and the investment benefits of enhanced international relations or access to knowledge that it brings, language does not fit exactly into a strictly economic cost–benefit framework. This is because, although it is a resource, its benefits are not as tangible or as measurable as those of minerals or agricultural products. Language is a social rather than an economic commodity.

In our context, therefore, language planning should be confined to the formulation of a set of principles that allow an optimal utilisation of the language(s) in a country for the benefit of all its citizens, and to manipulation of the relevant language(s) so that they have the capabilities required to fulfil all the communicative and other needs of the speakers. As with language empowerment, language planning has two aspects, the ideological and the technical. The former deals with policy decisions, and therefore concerns mainly decision-makers, while the latter deals with implementation of the policies. In what follows we shall discuss each of these aspects and the extent to which African countries have managed to make optimal use of their languages.

Ideological planning

Ideological planning usually starts with a policy decision. This is the stage at which the decision-makers have to make an explicit pronouncement about the language policy of the country. The policy should state clearly which language will be used for government business, public administration, education, science, mass media, diplomacy, international relations, legal matters, commerce, trade, social services and so on. The policy decision can be based on linguistic research and consultation, or it may be mere political decree.

Unfortunately, few African countries are explicit in their ideological planning. As Bamgbose (1991: 111) has rightly pointed out, most decisions and policies are 'characterised by one or more of the following problems: avoidance, vagueness, arbitrariness, fluctuation, and declaration without implementation.' Moreover, even where there are explicit language policies, as in Tanzania, Kenya, Botswana, Namibia or South Africa, they are not based on linguistic research or consultation but on government decree. Many concentrate on the ex-colonial and major languages. It is unusual for roles to be accorded to the minority languages; in fact, such languages tend to be ignored completely.

Once the decision-makers have decided which language or languages will be used for which functions, the next task is to create positive attitudes (as part of a process of 'sensitisation') towards the languages or standard forms that have been selected. Again, in most African countries, little sensitisation of the people is attempted when important policy decisions are made. Sensitisation of a population on matters of language and culture should be tied to the whole question of nationalism, national identity and unity. If this is done, and when all the indigenous languages are involved in the formulation of a language policy, it becomes easier for a government to demonstrate to the people its true commitment to ensuring the participation of all citizens. Mass mobilisation in the name of nationalism was carried out vigorously during the socialist regimes in Tanzania, Ethiopia and Somalia. This is one of the reasons why Kiswahili, Amharic and Somali, respectively, were able to entrench themselves so successfully in these countries. They are the only languages in Africa, apart from Arabic and Afrikaans, to be used in most of the secondary domains in their respective countries.

Technical planning

The technical aspect of language planning has two areas, namely norm and capacity planning. *Norm planning* involves, first, the selection of the variety or dialect which will be made the standard form of the language. Normally one selects the variety that is most prestigious, demographically the most important, the most centrally situated or the variety that is used in the capital city. Although the decision is usually based on technical considerations, the decision-makers often tend to have a stake in it. Thus, in the case of Kiswahili, Kiunguja, the dialect spoken in Zanzibar, was selected rather than Kimvita, the dialect of Mombasa, mainly for technical reasons, although the decision later had political implications.

The next step in norm planning is *codification*, which involves documentation of the chosen norms through the designing of a standard orthography, preparation of a reference grammar, compilation of a standard dictionary and the creation of a standard pronunciation manual. In most African countries there is reasonably adequate documentation only for the major languages. For the minority languages there is often nothing at all, or unreliable documents prepared by non-linguists such as missionaries and colonial enthusiasts. This is one area where linguists need to do a lot of work in preparing documentation, particularly for the small languages, many of which are highly threatened. Once there is documentation in a given language, it should be disseminated to the speakers for their use. At the same time a programme of literacy has to be introduced to enable people to read in their own language. In fact, as reported by Visser (2000) in the case of Naro, the speakers of many small languages become enthusiastic when they see their language written down in the same way as the more extensively used languages. Such a development empowers them as they gain confidence and feel a sense of equality with the others.

The other technical aspect of language planning is *capacity planning*. This involves the deliberate engineering of a language to make it capable of handling new functions. Since most African languages have traditionally been used mainly in village and rural settings and for cultural purposes, they have to be extended if they are to be used for more formal technical, official or national functions. These more formal functions may include education, science, technology, law, medicine and commerce, where unfamiliar concepts are involved.

The first stage in capacity planning is *language elaboration*, in which new terms are created, new idioms or jargons are established to be used in specific fields, a more appropriate orthography is designed and new grammatical rules or constructions are established to deal with the more complex requirements of formal or technical language use. Also, new semantic refinements have to be implemented to deal with possible ambiguities. In Africa, most elaboration activities have been carried out by language centres or academies (where they exist) or institutes of education as part of curriculum development activities. However, in most cases they have focused on the dominant languages because these are the languages whose roles have expanded upwards. Very little or no elaboration work has been done on the minority languages. It is worth noting, however, that some countries like Namibia, which has resolved to introduce primary education in mother tongues, have made substantial strides in the elaboration of the indigenous languages. Namibia has carried out useful school elaboration activities at the National Institute of Education Development (NIED) in Okahandja. Unfortunately, many African governments are not prepared to spend money on programmes of language documentation as they are not priority areas.

Once the process of language elaboration is far advanced, a new activity has to be introduced in the work of capacity planning, and that is *stylistic cultivation*. Since the language of law is not the same as the language of medicine, or the language of journalism is not the same as that of politics, it is important that specialised vocabulary, expressions and specific registers are established to create stylistic variation. English is able to distinguish between words with the same meaning but with different stylistic senses, such as proof (scientific), evidence (sociological), testimony (legal/religious) and symptom (medical). Often, languages that have borrowed from other languages develop such distinctions, and the borrowed terms would be the formal ones, with the indigenous or internally created forms as informal terms. For example, for 'engineer' Kiswahili has *injinia* (very formal, from English), *mhandisi* (less formal, from Arabic), and *fundi-mitambo* (informal, a compound of words of Bantu origin). Most minority languages would not have such a facility. However, this does not mean that they have no stylistic marking in their discourse.

This discussion has shown that not much has been done in the African countries in respect of ideological and technical language planning. Where there has been such planning, it has concentrated on the dominant languages as they are the ones that have been accorded higher roles in administration, education, parliament, courts of law or politics. Minority languages are in most cases not included in the ideological planning and therefore do not form part of the technical planning. This is unfortunate as it is the minority languages that are in need of much attention in codification, elaboration and cultivation processes, not only for their records but also as part of their empowerment.

Institutional Support for Language Empowerment

The role of institutions

If the African languages are to be empowered so that they are able not only to maintain themselves but also to flourish as effective media for their users and vehicles of their solidarity and self-identity, there is a need for concerted institutional support. This support should involve logistic and material contributions from the respective governments, regional and continent-wide organisations, non-governmental bodies and regional associations and societies.

The role of governments

In spite of the many resolutions passed by African countries at meetings of the former OAU (now AU), not much has been accomplished in the way of promotion and active use of African languages for formal and technical use. As indicated earlier, only Egypt and Libya use their selected indigenous languages as sole official languages. Much, therefore, needs to be done not only to elevate the dominant languages to assume official functions but also to promote the minority languages so that they too contribute to national development at different levels. Some of the measures that need to be taken by governments are set out below.

- Formulation of appropriate language policies that spell out which language will be used for which roles; provision of a schedule of implementation; and the establishment of a government department specifically to oversee implementation. The language policy should be based on objective research and arrived at after thorough national consultation.
- Establishment of active national councils or academies to deal with policy matters concerning language promotion and development. At present, few countries have a language council and, where they do exist, they are not very active as they are made up of civil servants and professionals who do not give the council's business much attention.
- Creation of language research centres which should be mandated to conduct language surveys, deal with matters of codification, elaboration and cultivation, and advise the language councils on issues of language promotion and development.
- Provision of support and finance for an extensive programme of documentation of all languages in the country. The programme should include orthographic design, compilation of dictionaries, preparation of reference grammars and the preparation of texts in the languages for educational and literacy purposes.

- Introduction of education in the mother tongue(s), particularly at the elementary level of education and for literacy work. In fact, a mother tongue can be used together with the major language in a bilingual form of education, as has been successfully carried out in some parts of New Zealand with Maori groups (Spolsky, 1989).
- Sensitisation and cultivation in people of a sense of pride in their languages, which they should come to view as resources and means by which they can participate in national affairs.

All this can be done only if African governments manifest a genuine political will and take active steps to implement a language policy once it has been formulated. The first step they have to take is to convince themselves of the national benefits that would be gained by promoting indigenous languages. As stated above, these include the participation of all citizens in the country's affairs, the practice of full democracy and the institution of human rights and equality in matters of education and information flow.

The role of regional and continent-wide bodies

A number of regional and continent-wide bodies have played important roles, at different times and with varying degrees of success, in the promotion or development of African languages. Since the inception of the Organisation of African Unity in 1963, there has been a great desire to promote the African languages. Article 29 of the OAU Charter, which was approved in 1986, states that the 'the working languages of the Organization are, if possible, African languages as well as English, Arabic, French and Portuguese'. However, until very recently only the head of state of Ethiopia had used Amharic at an OAU meeting (ACALAN 2002: 1). During the African Union summit held in Addis Ababa in July 2004, some heads of state from eastern Africa used Kiswahili to address the conference. These leaders included President Benjamin Mkapa of Tanzania and President Joachim Chissano of Mozambique.

Another manifestation of the OAU's desire to promote African languages was the creation of the Inter-African Bureau of Languages (BIL/OAU) in Kampala in the 1970s. Its main function was to implement the OAU's resolutions on matters of language and to prepare action plans. In 1986 the Bureau prepared a very comprehensive document, the 'Language Plan for Africa' (ACALAN, 2002: 2), in which it was recommended that Kiswahili be one of the working languages of the OAU. The plan did not have any visible effect, nor was Kiswahili actively used as a working language of the OAU. The Bureau itself was closed in 1987 for lack of funds.

Moreover, the Panafrican Association of Linguists, which was to provide professional advice to the OAU on matters of language promotion, has never taken off the ground since its formation in the mid-1990s. Many recent treaties, such as the Abuja Treaty of 1991 establishing the African Economic Community, have disregarded the proposed use of African languages as working languages (ACALAN 2002: 1). No intergovernmental meetings, even at regional level, have ever used an African language (apart from Arabic) as a working language. Even with the declaration that was made at the Decade of Education in Africa Conference held in Harare, Zimbabwe, in 1997, on the use of African languages in education, there have been no visible developments. The declaration has remained a mere conference record, kept in the relevant ministries of education.

The treaty of Lomé, Togo, establishing the African Union in 2000, has re-introduced the idea of using African languages as working languages of the newly renamed body. Hence, the Academy of Languages was established in February 2002, based in Bamako, Mali. Major tasks assigned to this body include the harmonisation of language policies and orthographies in Africa, the co-ordination of research on the African languages of the continent, the establishing of a database on the African languages and the promotion of cross-border languages. The big question here is whether the Academy will succeed where so many attempts over the last 40 years have failed. Certainly, the newly created African Union has a major role to play in the promotion and effective use of the indigenous languages. However, its efforts can only succeed if there is full commitment on the part of African leaders.

Since the 1970s a number of regional bodies have been created in many parts of Africa to deal with both language and cultural issues. These include: CICIBA (International Centre of Bantu Civilisation) in Libreville; EACROTANAL (Eastern African Centre for Research on Oral Traditions and African National Languages) in Zanzibar; CELHTO (Centre for Research on Languages, History and Oral Traditions) in Niamey; CERDO-TOLA (Regional Centre for Documentation of Oral Traditions and African Languages) in Yaunde; ICA (African Cultural Institute) in Dakar; and BASE (African Centre for Educational Studies) in Kinshasa. All these centres are charged with the mission of studying the languages and cultures of the relevant regions as part of the African heritage and also as a means of empowering the languages concerned. However, despite all the dedication of the personnel recruited to run these centres, very little has been accomplished for lack of financial and logistic support from the member states. Many, indeed, have become dormant.

Although Africa would have benefited from collective action at continental and regional levels on the development of its languages, the many efforts that have been made over the last 40 years have, sadly, remained at conference level. A stronger and more honest political will is needed from African governments. If the New Economic and Political Agenda for Development (NEPAD) is to succeed, it will need to transpose the economic and technological tools in use elsewhere in the world into African cultural and linguistic contexts so as to reach the common people.

The role of non-governmental organisations

A number of non-governmental organisations have shown interest in the promotion of indigenous languages. UNESCO has been in the forefront since its declaration in 1953 that education should, as far as possible, be given in a mother tongue – especially in the early years of child development – for both cognitive and affective reasons (UNESCO, 1953).

In more recent years, UNESCO has shown great concern over the question of endangered languages. At its General Assembly of November 1993, it is reported by Crystal (2000: vii) that the meeting adopted the 'Endangered Languages Project', including the 'Red Book of Endangered Languages'. Then, in 1995, an International Clearing House for Endangered Languages was inaugurated at the University of Tokyo. (Dwyer *et al.*, 2003). That same year an Endangered Languages Fund was instituted in the USA, coinciding with the establishment of a Foundation for Endangered Languages in the United Kingdom. Furthermore, a major international gathering took place in 2003 in Paris, France, at which international experts met to consider the issues of safeguarding the endangered languages. All this was part of the UNESCO programme known as 'Safeguarding of the Endangered Languages' that has been instituted by the Intangible Cultural Heritage Section of UNESCO. At most of these events the major concern has been that, although languages have died off throughout history, the current rate of extinction has become alarming. Thus, there is a universal upsurge of both professional and public concern.

At the conclusion of the Paris meeting, held in March 2003, at which many language experts had gathered to look for ways of safeguarding the endangered languages, the following recommendations were made to the Director-General of UNESCO with regard to the measures to be taken by member states:

- Each member state should survey and profile those languages which were found to be endangered.
- Each member state should actively promote recognition of the endangered languages of their countries.

- Each member state should encourage the documentation of endangered languages.
- Each member state should create conditions that facilitate the active use of, and access to, endangered languages. *Inter alia*, this includes assigning all relevant languages their rightful place in the educational system and media and ensuring access to cyberspace. Such interventions should be subject to the wishes of individual speech communities, respecting their entitlement to linguistic human rights.
- Each member state should foster the pride of speech communities in their own language and culture, as well as secure equal prestige for all languages present in the state.
- Each member state should explore the economic and social benefits of linguistic and cultural diversity as a stimulus to sustainable development.
- Each member state should provide, where feasible, and with assistance from the international community, funding for documentation and programmes to revitalise and strengthen endangered languages.

Certainly these recommendations are well thought out and, if implemented, would go a long way to identifying, documenting, promoting and revitalising endangered languages in various countries of the world. However, at the implementation level the recommendations would only succeed if the relevant countries give priority to minority language issues, just as they do to other critical issues like HIV/AIDS, environmental degeneration and poverty.

Apart from the remarkable steps taken by UNESCO, a number of foundations and research organisations have, in recent years, also supported symposia and research on the endangered languages. These organisations include the Volkswagen Foundation (Volkswagenstiftung), the Daimler Chrysler Foundation and the German Research Foundation, as well as other agencies such as SAREC and NORAD.

Moreover, a programme known as the Endangered Languages Documentation Programme has been established at the School of Oriental and African Studies (SOAS) in London with the aim of collecting as much information as possible on endangered languages and documenting it before the languages become extinct. The programme includes graduate studies in language surveys and documentation. The Summer Institute of Linguistics and the Lutheran Bible Translators have carried out extensive sociolinguistic and descriptive research in many parts of the world, including Africa, with the aim of establishing orthographies and reference materials. Although their ultimate aim is the preparation of religious materials, including translation of the Bible, their work has proven very useful in the preservation and obtaining of linguistic records for these languages. In more recent years, some local non-governmental organisations have also been established to deal with the question of African language promotion and empowerment. These include the Open Society Initiative of Southern Africa (OSISA) and the Centre for Advanced Studies on African Society (CASAS), both based in southern Africa. Their major aim is to contribute to finding regional solutions to the language problems of the relevant countries.

It would appear from the foregoing that there is tremendous concern, particularly at the international level, about the endangered languages of the world. A considerable amount of logistic and material support seems to be readily available. The main problem now is how to channel such concern into the various countries so as to establish systematic measures to deal with the problem of language endangerment.

Societies and associations

In some parts of Africa there are professional societies and associations concerned with, among other things, the promotion, development and effective use of the indigenous languages. These societies include the West Africa Linguistic Society (WALS), the Linguistic Association for SADC Universities (LASU), and the African Languages Association of Southern Africa (ALASA). They too have realised the need to deal with the problem of language endangerment, which has led to them paying more attention to sociolinguistic research as well as conducting primary research on individual languages. At conferences there are usually para-sessions on the endangered languages.

Elsewhere in the world, linguistic associations have realised the urgency of addressing the problem of endangered languages. The Permanent International Congress of Linguists (CIPL) is sponsoring a project on endangered languages, for which it has obtained UNESCO support (Bamgbose, 2000: 41). The World Congress of African Linguistics (WOCAL) has organised special sessions on endangered languages at its congresses and has indicated in its constitution the primary need to promote and empower the indigenous languages.

At the same time, the Linguistic Society of America (LSA) has recognised the importance of documenting and preserving the linguistic diversity of the world by observing that 'if the central concern of linguistics is essentially anthropological and psychological, i.e. to provide insight into the nature of "humanness" through investigation of the structure of human language, then linguistics will without question benefit by supporting research on the documentation of dying or endangered languages' (Linguistic Society of America, 1996). Evidently, the study of universal grammar and linguistic typology cannot be complete or revealing if it does not take into account some of the unique features and diversities found in some of the most 'exotic' languages. Latin and ancient Greek, for example, continue to provide useful data for linguists, thanks to the fact that they were well documented before their 'demise'. At the 1995 meeting of the Committee on Endangered Languages and Their Preservation in New Orleans, Louisiana, a survey was proposed on the endangered languages on which the members of the Linguistics Society of America had worked or were working. With the collaboration of other linguistic societies, they prepared questionnaires for conducting surveys, particularly on the endangered languages of the USA, where at least 150 such languages are highly endangered. Other organisations that are collaborating in the initiative include the German Linguistic Group, the International Clearing House for Endangered Languages in Tokyo and the Society for the Study of the Indigenous Languages of the Americas (SSILA).

The Future of the African Languages

The future of the African Languages, particularly the endangered minority languages, depends very much on the extent to which collective action can be mobilised that involves both local and external expertise and resources and has the support of the respective governments. These efforts should, ideally, be co-ordinated by the language experts from each country. Such experts should be given every opportunity both to liaise with the relevant authorities in the government and to correspond with outside organisations, donors and individuals. The work should consist of thorough sociolinguistic and descriptive research on these languages, with the aim of producing orthographies, reference grammars and dictionaries/glossaries. As was rightly pointed out by Larry Hyman in his keynote speech at the opening ceremony of the Fourth World Congress of African Linguists in June 2003 at Rutgers University, USA, it is now time for African linguists to give priority to descriptive or primary research on African languages rather than focusing on theoretical and abstract research with little or no utilitarian value to the African countries and the continent as a whole (Hyman, 2003).

A project that is currently under way in Tanzania, the 'Languages of Tanzania Project', could serve as a model. This project, which is being carried out mainly by Tanzanian linguists with the collaboration of foreign scholars, is aimed at describing the Tanzanian languages, with the goal of preparing orthographies, reference grammars and dictionaries/glossaries on the more than 120 languages in the country. Some of the information will be kept in a special database. The documents so prepared will not only serve as records of the languages but will also be used to sensitise the speakers to the value of their languages, thus creating positive attitudes towards them.

Summary and Conclusions

One of the ways to ensure that the endangered and other minority languages maintain themselves and continue to be vibrant is to empower them. Language empowerment is effected by the institutionalisation of measures to elevate a language's social status and to make it capable of handling public domains. The measures to be instituted are ideological and technical. While the ideological measures are the responsibility of the decision-makers, the technical measures concern mainly language experts.

In order to carry out a systematic process of language empowerment, languages have to undergo language planning, which involves the formulation of a set of principles that allow an optimal utilisation of the language(s) in a country for the benefit of all its citizens and the manipulation of the relevant language(s) to have the necessary capability of fulfilling all the communicative and other needs of the speakers. Unfortunately, most countries in Africa have not had any systematic language planning, as they have not given much priority to language questions.

Responding to the alarming rate at which languages are becoming extinct, many external organisations and foundations are now offering strong support to deal with the problem of language death. Many professionals and professional organisations are also keen to deal with the problem. It is unfortunate, therefore, that few African governments have paid much heed to the language issues of the continent. Discussions and resolutions tend to go no further than the conference table because many African leaders lack the political will to implement the steps necessary to promote and make effective use of the indigenous languages.

Action should involve local experts in co-ordinating research activities in their respective countries. Tanzania has provided a model through the Languages of Tanzania Project. It is imperative that, as a matter of urgency, each African country takes the language problem seriously and adopts appropriate measures in the same way that measures are being taken to preserve biodiversity.

However, any measures to empower the speakers of a language that do not involve the speakers themselves are unlikely to succeed or be sustained.

The speakers must be part of the process. Thus, projects, like the Kuru Development Trust for Naro in Botswana and the Molteno Project for Ju|'hoan in Namibia have been highly successful because of the involvement of those who actually use the language. Likewise, in southern Africa there is now a network of working groups in which the Khoesan speakers themselves are involved, known as the Working Group of Indigenous Minorities of Southern Africa (WIMSA). The formation of such groups that bring the speakers of a language on board in dealing with their language should be encouraged in other African regions.

It is worth noting here that, by preserving and empowering the minority languages alongside the dominant languages, African countries would be promoting true democracy and equality. One of the sources of political conflict in Africa is the fact that some ethnic groups are not granted full participation in their country's affairs. Although the political and ethnic conflicts in countries like Liberia, Sierra Leone, the Central African Republic, Côte d'Ivoire, the Democratic Republic of Congo, the Congo Republic and Angola stem from a variety of socio-historical, economic and ethnic grievances, a key feature in their perpetuation is linguistic inequality. Once such inequalities are addressed, the other differences would be substantially minimised as the speakers of the various languages would feel that they are recognised and valued in the country's affairs.

Finally, it is gratifying to see the many concerns and efforts that have been made to preserve the minority languages in the form of documentation of their linguistic, cultural and artistic features. It is important that such work be co-ordinated in order to make the optimal use of resources and to ensure maximum coverage of the most critically endangered languages. Wherever possible, it is desirable to empower the relevant languages and their speakers through publications in the language, the institution of literacy and education in the mother tongue, and by raising the social status of the speakers. On the other hand, the choice of whether to maintain their language or shift to another remains an exclusive right of the community concerned as it must be free to choose whether to shift so as to benefit from the privileges enjoyed by the majority language speakers, or whether to continue using the mother tongue for reasons of both self-identity and self-determination.

References

Abdulaziz-Mkilifi, M.H. (1978) Triglossia and Swahili–English bilingualism in Tanzania. In J.A. Fishman (ed.) *Advances in the Study of Societal Multilingualism* (pp. 129–49). The Hague: Mouton de Gruyter.

Academy of Languages (ACALAN) (2002) *From the Mission of the African Academy of Languages to the African Academy of Languages*. Bamako: African Academy of Languages.

Acquaye, Alfred, A. (1968) *Children of West Africa*. New York: Sterling; London: Oak Tree Press.

ADEA Working Group (1996a) The role of African languages in education and sustainable development. *Association of the Development of Education in Africa Newsletter* 8 (4), 1–4.

ADEA Working Group (1996b) Languages of instruction and language policies: A synthesis of research. *Association of the Development of Education in Africa Newsletter* 8 (4), 5–7.

Adegbija, E. (1994) *Language Attitudes in Sub-Saharan Africa: A Sociolinguistic Overview*. Clevedon: Multilingual Matters.

Alexandre, P. (1967) *Langues et langage en Afrique noire*. Paris: Payot.

Auburger, L. (1990) Linguistic minority relations. *Sociolinguistica* 4, 169–90.

Baker, C. (1992) *Attitudes and Language*. Clevedon: Multilingual Matters.

Bamgbose, A. (1991) *Language and the Nation: The Language Question in Sub-Saharan Africa*. Edinburgh: Edinburgh University Press.

Bamgbose, A. (2000) *Language and Exclusion: The Consequences of Language Policies in Africa*. London: Transaction Publishers.

Barton, H.D. (1980) Language use among Ilala residents. In E. Polomé and C.P. Hill (eds) *Language in Tanzania* (pp. 176–205). Oxford: Oxford University Press.

Batibo, H.M. (1992) The fate of ethnic languages in Tanzania. In M. Brenzinger (ed.) *Language Death: Factual and Theoretical Explorations, with Special Reference to East Africa* (pp. 85–98). Berlin: Mouton de Gruyter.

Batibo, H.M. (1997) The fate of the minority languages of Botswana. In B. Smieja and M. Tasch (eds) *Human Contact through Language and Linguistics* (pp. 243–52). Frankfurt: Peter Lang.

Batibo, H.M. (1998) The fate of the Khoesan language of Botswana. In M. Brenzinger (ed.) *Endangered Languages in Africa* (pp. 267–84) Köln: Rüdiger Köppe Verlag.

Batibo, H.M. (2000) The sounds of Africa: Their phonetic characteristics. In V. Webb and K. Sure (eds) *African Voices: An Introduction to African Languages and Linguistics* (pp. 133–59). Pretoria: Oxford University Press of Southern Africa.

Batibo, H.M. (2001a) The empowerment of minority languages for education and development. In R. Trewby and S. Fitchat (eds) *Language and Development in Southern Africa: Making the Right Choices* (pp. 123–35). Windhoek: Gamsberg Macmillan.

Batibo, H.M. (2001b) The endangered languages of Africa: A case study from Botswana. In L. Maffi (ed.) *Language Knowledge and the Environment: The Interdependence of Biological and Cultural Diversity* (pp. 311–24). Washington: Smithsonian Institution Press.

Batibo, H.M. (2003a) The role of external setting in language shift process: The case of the Nama-speaking Ovaherero in Tsabong. Paper presented at the 4th World Congress of African Linguistics, Rutgers University, USA, 17–22 June, 2003.

Batibo, H.M. (2003b) The marked bilingualism model and its relevance to Africa. Paper presented at a linguistics seminar, University of Manchester, UK, 11 November 2003.

Batibo, H.M. and Mosaka, M.N. (2000) Linguistic barriers as a hindrance to information flow: The case of Botswana. In H.M. Batibo and B. Smieja (eds) *Botswana: The Future of the Minority Languages* (pp. 95–104). Frankfurt: Peter Lang.

Batibo, H.M. and Smieja, B. (eds) (2000) *Botswana: The Future of the Minority Languages.* Frankfurt: Peter Lang.

Batibo, H.M. and Tsonope, J. (2000) Language vitality among the Nama of Tsabong. In H.M. Batibo and J. Tsonope (eds) *The State of Khoesan Languages in Botswana* (pp. 49–58). Gaborone: Tasalls Publishing and Books.

Bender, M.L. (2000) Nilo-Saharan. In B. Heine and D. Nurse (eds) *African Languages: An Introduction* (pp. 43–73). Cambridge: Cambridge University Press.

Blench, R. (1998) The status of the languages of central Nigeria. In M. Brenzinger (ed.) *Endangered Languages in Africa* (pp. 187–206). Köln: Rüdiger Köppe Verlag.

Bobaljik, J.D., Pensalfini, R. and Storto, L. (eds) (1996) *Papers on Language Endangerment and the Maintenance of Linguistic Diversity.* Cambridge, MA: MIT Working Papers in Linguistics.

Brenzinger, M. (ed.) (1992) *Language Death: Factual and Theoretical Explorations, with Special Reference to East Africa.* Berlin: Mouton de Gruyter.

Brenzinger, M. (ed.) (1998) *Endangered Languages in Africa.* Köln: Rüdiger Köppe Verlag.

Brenzinger, M. and Heine, B. (1995) *The Mukodogo Maasai: An Ethnobotanical Survey.* Köln: Rüdiger Köppe Verlag.

Calteaux, K. (1994) Sociolinguistic analysis of a multilingual community. PhD thesis, Rand Afrikaans University.

Carnie, A. (1996) Modern Irish: A case study in language revival failure. In J.D. Bobaljik, R. Pensalfini and L. Storto (eds) *Papers on Language Endangerment and the Maintenance of Linguistic Diversity* (pp. 99–114). Cambridge, MA: MIT Working Papers in Linguistics.

Chebanne, A. and Nthapelelang, M. (2000) The sociolinguistic survey of the Eastern Khoe in the Boteti and Makgadikgadi Pans area of Botswana. In H.M. Batibo and B. Smieja (eds) *Botswana: The Future of the Minority Languages* (pp. 79–94). Frankfurt: Peter Lang.

Childs, G.T. (2003) Language death within Atlantic: Survival strategies and language change. Paper presented at the 4th World Congress of African Linguistics, Rutgers University, USA, June 17–22, 2003.

Clements, N.G. (2000) Phonology. In B. Heine and D. Nurse (eds) *African Languages: An Introduction* (pp. 123–60). Cambridge: Cambridge University Press.

Cole, D.T. (1995) *Setswana: Animals and Plants.* Gaborone: Botswana Society.
Committee of Endangered Languages and Their Preservation (CELTP) (1994) The need for the documentation of linguistic diversity. *Linguistic Society of America Bulletin* 144 (June), 5.
Connell, B. (1998) Moribund languages of the Nigerian–Cameroon Borderland. In M. Brenzinger (ed.) *Endangered Languages in Africa* (pp. 207–28). Köln: Rüdiger Köppe Verlag.
Coulmas, F. (1983) Languages of the World. *Development Forum* 91 (August–September), 2–4.
Crawhall, N. (1997) The death of a 'useless' language. *Mail and Guardian*, 23–29 May 1997, Johannesburg.
Crawhall, N. (1998) Report on the Molteno Project: Breakthrough to J|'hoan. Grade 1 Materials Development Workshop, Okahandja, Namibia, 2–4 December 1998.
Crystal, D. (1997) *The Cambridge Encyclopedia* (3rd edn). Cambridge: Cambridge University Press.
Crystal, D. (2000). *Language Death.* Cambridge: Cambridge University Press.
Darwin, C. (1859) *The Origin of Species.* London: Murray.
Diamond, J. (1993) Speaking with a single tongue. *Discover* (February), 78–85.
Dimmendaal, G.J. (1989) On language death in Eastern Africa. In N. Dorian (ed.) *Investigating Obsolescence: Studies in Language Contraction and Death* (pp. 13–31). Cambridge: Cambridge University Press.
Dimmendaal, G.J. (1992) Reduction in Kore reconsidered. In M. Brenzinger (ed.) *Language Death: Factual and Theoretical Explorations, with Special Reference to East Africa* (pp. 117–36). Berlin: Mouton de Gruyter.
Dimmendaal, G.J. (1998) Language contraction versus other types of contact-induced change. In M. Brenzinger (ed.) *Endangered Languages in Africa* (pp. 71–118). Köln: Rüdiger Köppe Verlag.
Dimmendaal, G.J. (2000) Morphology. In B. Heine and D. Nurse (eds) *African Languages: An Introduction* (pp. 161–93). Cambridge: Cambridge University Press.
Dorian, N.C. (1977) The problem of the semi-speaker in language death. In W.U. Dressler and R. Wodak–Kodotter (eds) *Language Death* (International Journal of the Sociology of Language 12) (pp. 23–32). Paris: Mouton Publishers.
Dorian, N.C. (1998) Western language ideologies and small language prospects. In L. Grenoble and L.J. Whaley (eds) *Endangered Languages: Current Issues and Future Prospects* (pp. 3–21). Cambridge: Cambridge University Press.
Dressler, W.U. (1972) On the phonology of language death. In *Papers from the Eighth Regional Meeting of the Chicago Linguistic Society* (pp. 448–57). Chicago: Chicago Linguistic Society.
Dwyer, A., Brenzinger, M. and Yamamoto, A.Y. (2003) Safeguarding of endangered languages: Report on the Project of the Intangible Cultural Heritage Section of UNESCO. *The Endangered Languages Fund Newsletter* 7, 1–4.
Edwards, J. (1992) Sociopolitical aspects of language maintenance and loss: Towards a typology of minority language situations. In W. Fase, K. Jaspaert and S. Kroon (eds) *Maintenance and Loss of Minority Languages* (pp. 37–54). Amsterdam and Philadelphia: John Benjamins.
Ehret, C. (1980) *The Historical Reconstruction of Southern Cushitic Phonology and Vocabulary.* Berlin: Dietrich Reiner.
Erny, P. (1973) *Childhood and Cosmos. The Social Psychology of the Black African Child.* London: Blackwell.

Fishman, J.A. (1971) The impact of nationalism in language planning. In J. Rubin and B. Jernudd (eds) *Can Language be Planned? Sociolinguistic Theory and Practice for Developing Nations* (pp. 3–20). Hawaii: University Press of Hawaii.

Fishman, J.A. (1974) *Advances of Language Planning.* The Hague: Mouton de Gruyter.

Fishman, J.A. (1991) *Reversing Language Shift: Theoretical and Empirical Foundations of Assistance to Threatened Languages.* Clevedon: Multilingual Matters.

Froger, T. (1910) *Etude sur la langue des mossi, suivie d'un vocabulaire et de textes.* Paris: Leroux.

Gal, S. (1979) *Language Shift: Social Determinants of Linguistic Change in Bilingual Austria.* New York: Academic Press.

Goldsmith, J. (1990) *Autosegmental and Metrical Phonology.* Oxford: Blackwell.

Greenberg, J.H. (1963) *Languages of Africa.* Indiana: Indiana University Press.

Greenberg, J.H. (1971) Urbanism, migration, and language. In J. Greenberg and A. Dil (eds) *Language, Culture and Communication* (pp. 198–211). Stanford: Stanford University Press.

Grenoble, L.A. and Whaley, L.J. (1998) Towards a typology of language endangerment. In L.A. Grenoble and L.J. Whaley (eds) *Endangered Languages: Language Loss and Community Response* (pp. 22–54). Cambridge: Cambridge University Press.

Grice, H.P. (1975) Logic and conversation. In P. Cole and J. Morgan (eds) *Syntax and Semantics: Speech Acts* (pp. 54–72). New York: Academic Press.

Grimes, B.F. (ed.) (2000) *Ethnologue: Languages of the World* (Vols 1 and 2, 14th edn). Dallas: SIL International.

Gueldemann, T. and Vossen, R. (2000) The Khoisan languages. In B. Heine and D. Nurse (eds) *African Languages: An Introduction* (pp. 99–122). Cambridge: Cambridge University Press.

Haarmann, H. (2001) *Die Kleinsprachen der Welt-Existenzbedrohung und Überlebenschancen. Eine umfassende Dokumentation.* Frankfurt: Peter Lang.

Hachipola, S.J. (1996) *Survey of the Minority Languages of Zimbabwe.* Harare: Department of African Languages and Literature, University of Zimbabwe.

Hayward, R.J. (1998) The endangered languages of Ethiopia: What's at stake for the linguist? In M. Brenzinger (ed.) *Endangered Languages in Africa* (pp. 17–38). Köln: Rüdiger Köppe Verlag.

Hayward, R.J. (2000) Afro-Asiatic. In B. Heine and D. Nurse (eds) *African Languages: An Introduction* (pp. 74–98). Cambridge: Cambridge University Press.

Heine, B. (1970) *Status and Use of African Lingua Francas.* München: Weltforum Verlag.

Heine, B. (1990) Language policy in Africa. In B. Weinstein (ed.) *Language and Political Development* (pp. 167–89). Norwood: Ablex Publishing Corp.

Heine, B. and Legère, K. (1995) *Swahili Plant Names: An Ethnobotanical Survey.* Köln: Rüdiger Köppe Verlag.

Heine, B. and Nurse, D. (2000) Introduction. In B. Heine and D. Nurse (eds) *African Languages: An Introduction.* Cambridge: Cambridge University Press.

Hyman, L. (2003) Why describe African languages? Keynote address to the 4th World Congress of African Linguistics, Rutgers University, 17–22 June, 2003.

Ibekwe, P. (ed.) (1998) *Wit and Wisdom of Africa: Proverbs from Africa and the Caribbean.* Oxford: Worldview

Idris, H.F. (2003) The status and use of African languages vs. Arabic in Sudan. Paper presented at the 4th World Congress of African Linguistics, Rutgers University, 17–22 June 2003.

International African Institute (IAI) (1981) *Provisional Survey of the Major Languages and Language Use in the Independent States of Sub-Saharan Africa*. Paris: UNESCO.

Irvine, J. (1974) Strategies and status manipulation in the Wolof greeting. In R. Bauman and J. Schirzer (eds) *Explorations in the Ethnography of Speaking* (pp. 35–49). London: Cambridge university Press.

Jernudd, B. and Das Gupta, J. (1971) Language planning in developing nations. In J. Rubin and B. Jernudd (eds) *Can Languages be Planned? Sociolinguistic Theory and Practice for Developing Nations* (pp. 195–215). Honolulu: The University Press of Hawaii.

Kagame, A. (1956) *La philosophie bantu–rwandaise de l'être*. Bruxelles: Académie Royale des Sciences Coloniales.

Kapanga, A. (1998) Impact of language variation and accommodation theory on language maintenance: An analysis of Shaba Swahili. In L.A. Grenoble and L.J. Whaley (eds) *Endangered Languages: Current Issues and Future Prospects* (pp. 134–49). Cambridge: Cambridge University Press.

Katzner, K. (2000) *The Languages of the World*. London, Routledge.

Krapf, L. and Rebman, J. (1887) *A Nika–English Dictionary*. London: Society for the Promotion of Christian Knowledge.

Krauss, M. (1992) The world's languages in crisis. *Language* 68, 4–10.

Ladefoged, P. (1964) *A Phonetic Study of West African Languages*. Cambridge: Cambridge University Press.

Ladefoged, P. and Maddieson, I. (1996) *The Sounds of the World Languages*. Oxford: Blackwell.

Ladefoged, P., Glick, R. and Criper, C. (1972) *Language in Uganda*. London: Oxford University Press.

Laitin, D.D. (1992) *Language Repertoires and State Construction in Africa*. Cambridge: Cambridge University Press.

Laye, C. (1966) *L'enfant noir* (J.A. Hutchinson, ed.). Cambridge: Cambridge University Press.

Legère, K. (1992) Language shift in Tanzania. In M. Brenzinger (ed.) *Language Death: Factual and Theoretical Explorations, with Special Reference to East Africa* (pp. 99–118). Berlin: Mouton de Gruyter.

Le Page, R. (1964) *The National Language Question: Linguistic Problems of Newly Independent States*. New York: Oxford University Press.

Le Roux, W. (1999) *Torn Apart: San Children as Change Agents in a Process of Acculturation*. Ghanzi: Kuru Development Trust.

Linguistic Society of America (LSA) (1996) Policy statement: the need for the documentation of linguistic diversity. In J.D. Bobaljik, R. Pensalfini and L. Storto (eds) *Papers on Language Endangerment and the Maintenance of Linguistic Diversity* (pp. 181–2). Cambridge MA: MIT Working Papers in Linguistics.

Maddieson, I. (1984) *Patterns of Sounds*. Cambridge: Cambridge University Press.

Maffi, L. (ed.) (2001) *Language Knowledge and the Environment: The Interdependence of Biological and Cultural Diversity*. Washington: Smithsonian Institution Press.

Maho, J.F. (2004) How many languages are there in Africa, really? In K. Bromber and B. Smieja (eds) *African Languages and Globalisation: Risks and Benefits* (pp. 179–96). Berlin and New York: Mouton de Gruyter.

Mann, M. and Dalby, D. (eds) (1987) *A Thesaurus of African Languages*. London: Hans Zell.

Mazonde, I.N. (2002) The San in Botswana and the issue of subjectivities. In I.N. Mazonde (ed.) *Minorities in the Millennium: Perspectives for Botswana* (pp. 57–72). Gaborone: Botswana Printing and Publishing.

Mbiti, J.S. (1969) *African Religions and Philosophy.* London: Heinemann.

Mchombo, S. (1993) Introduction. In S. Mchombo (ed.) *Theoretical Aspects of Bantu Grammar* (pp. 1–16). Stanford: CSCI Publishers.

Mekacha, R. (1993) Is Tanzania diglossic? The status and role of community languages. (Mimeo).

Mkude, D. (2001) Minority languages vs Kiswahili in Tanzania: A painful dilemma. In R. Trewby and S. Fitchat (eds) *Language and Development in Southern Africa: Making the Right Choices* (pp. 159–70). Windhoek: Gamsberg Macmillan.

Myers-Scotton, C. (1992) Code-switching as a mechanism of deep borrowing, language shift, and language death. In M. Brenzinger (ed.) *Language Death: Factual and Theoretical Explorations, with Special Reference to East Africa* (pp. 31–58). Berlin: Mouton de Gruyter.

Myers-Scotton, C. (1993) *Social Motivations for Code-Switching: Evidence from Africa.* Oxford: Clarendon Press.

Ngugi wa Thiong'o, J. (1965) *The River Between.* London: Heinemann Educational Books.

Nketia, J.H.K. (1971) The linguistic aspect of style in African languages. In T.A. Sebeok (ed.) *Linguistics in Sub-Saharan Africa* (pp. 733–57) (Current Trends in Linguistics). The Hague and Paris: Mouton de Gruyter.

Nurse, D. (2000) *Inheritance, Contact, and Change in Two East African Languages* (Language Contact in Africa 4). Köln: Rüdiger Köppe Verlag.

Organization of African Unity (OAU) (1986) *Language Plan of Action for Africa.* Document CM/1352/XLIV. Addis Ababa: OAU Secretariat.

Ohuche, O. and Otaala, B. (eds) (1981) *The African Child and his Environment* (Science Education Programme for Africa). Oxford: Pergamon for the United Nations Environmental Programme.

Polomé, E. and Hill, C.P. (eds) *Language in Tanzania.* Oxford: Oxford University Press.

Pongweni, A. (2000) Figurative language, culture, and the problems of translation. In S.R. Makoni and N. Kamwangamalu (eds) *Language and Institutions in Africa* (CASAS Books Series No. 5) (pp. 131–48). Cape Town: Centre for Advanced Studies of African Societies.

Reh, M. (1981) Sprache und Gesellschaft. In B. Heine, T. Schadeberg and E. Wolff (eds) *Die Sprachen Afrikas* (pp. 513–57). Hamburg: Buske.

Robinson, C.D. (1996) *Language Use in Rural Development: An African Perspective.* The Hague: Mouton de Gruyter.

Rubanza, Y.I. (1994) Languages in Tanzania. (Mimeo)

Rubin, J. and B. Jernudd (eds) (1971) *Can Language be Planned? Sociolinguistic Theory and Practice for Developing Nations.* Honolulu: University Press of Hawaii.

Sapir, E. (1921) *Language.* New York: Harcourt, Brace and Jovanovich.

Sasse, H.-J. (1992) Theory of language death. In M. Brenzinger (ed.) *Language Death: Factual and Theoretical Explorations, with Special Reference to East Africa* (pp. 7–30). Berlin: Mouton de Gruyter.

Schadeberg, T. (1999) Katupha law in Makhuwa. In J.-M. Hombert and L. Hyman (eds) *Bantu Historical Linguistics: Theoretical and Empirical Perspectives* (pp. 379–411). Stanford: CSCI Publishers.

Selolwane, P.O. (1995) Ethnicity, development and the problems of social integration in Botswana: The case of Basarwa. (Mimeo).

Shimizu, K. (1978) The southern Bauchi group of Chadic languages – A survey report. *Africana Marburgensia* (special issue).

Slomanson, P. (1996) Explaining and revising the failure of the Irish language revision. In J.D. Bobaljik, R. Pensalfini and L. Storto (eds) *Papers on Language Endangerment and the Maintenance of Linguistic Diversity* (pp. 115–36). Cambridge, MA: MIT Working Papers in Linguistics.

Smied, J.F. (1991) *English in Africa: An Introduction*. London: Longman.

Smieja, B. (1999) Code-switching and language shift in Botswana: Indicators for language change and language death: A progress report. *ITL Review of Applied Linguistics* 123/124, 125–60.

Smieja, B. (2000) Code-switching in Botswana. Exception or rule? In H.M. Batibo and B. Smieja (eds) *Botswana: The Future of the Minority Languages* (pp. 153–76). Frankfurt: Peter Lang.

Smieja, B. (2003) *Language Pluralism in Botswana: Hope or Hurdle?* Frankfurt: Peter Lang.

Sommer, G. (1992) A survey on language death in Africa. In M. Brenzinger (ed.) *Language Death: Factual and Theoretical Explorations, with Special Reference to East Africa* (pp. 301–417). Berlin: Mouton de Gruyter.

Spolsky, B. (1989) Maori bilingual education and language revitalization. *Journal of Multilingual and Multicultural Development* 10 (2), 89–106.

Sure, K. (2000) Language in education and language learning in Africa. In V. Webb and K. Sure (eds) *African Voices: An Introduction to African Languages and Linguistics* (pp. 286–311). Pretoria: Oxford University Press of Southern Africa.

Sure, K. (2002) Language planning and national development in Kenya. In I. Rissom (ed.) *Language in Contact* (pp. 23–37). Bayreuth: Eckhard Breitinger.

Thomason, S.G. and T. Kaufman (1988) *Language Contact, Creolisation and Genetic Linguistics*. Berkeley: University of California Press.

Tosco, M. (1992) Dahalo: An endangered language. In M. Brenzinger (ed.) *Language Death: Factual and Theoretical Explorations, with Special Reference to East Africa* (pp. 137–56). Berlin: Mouton de Gruyter.

Traill, A. (1995) The Khoesan languages of South Africa. In R. Mesthrie (ed.) *Language and Social History* (Studies in South African Societies) (pp. 1–18). Cape Town: David Philip.

UNESCO (1953) *The Use of Vernacular Languages in Education* (Report of the UNESCO meeting of specialists). Paris: UNESCO.

UNESCO (2003a) *UNESCO Red Book of Endangered Languages: Africa* (data supplied by B. Heine and M. Brenzinger). Tokyo: International Clearing House for Endangered Languages (ICHEL). http://www.tooyoo.l.u-tokyo.ac.jp/Redbook/index.html.

UNESCO (2003b) Language vitality and endangerment. Available as pdf from the Endangered Languages page at http://portal.unesco.org/culture/en/ev.php-URL_ID=8270&URL_DO=DO_TOPIC&URL_SECTION=201.html.

Vakhtin, N.N. (1998) Copper Island Aleut: A case of language 'resurrection'. In L.A. Grenoble and L.J. Whaley (eds) *Endangered Languages: Current Issues and Future Prospects* (pp. 317–55). Cambridge: Cambridge University Press.

Visser, H. (2000) Language and cultural empowerment of the Khoesan people: The Naro experience. In H.M. Batibo and B. Smieja (eds) *Botswana: The Future of the Minority Languages* (pp. 193–215). Frankfurt: Peter Lang.

Watson, K. (1994) Caught between Scylla and Charybdis: Linguistics and the educational dilemma facing policy makers in pluralist states. *International Journal of Education* 37, 70–94.

Watters J.R. (2000) Syntax. In B. Heine and D. Nurse (eds) *African Languages: An Introduction* (pp. 194–230). Cambridge: Cambridge University Press.

Webb, V. and K. Sure (eds) (2000) *African Voices: An Introduction to African Languages and Linguistics*. Pretoria: Oxford University Press of Southern Africa.

Whiteley, W.H. (ed.) (1971) *Language Use and Social Change*. London: Oxford University Press for the International African Institute.

Whorf, B.L. (1956) *Language Thought and Reality: Selected Writings* (J.B. Carrol, ed.). Cambridge, MA: MIT Press.

Williamson, K. (2003) Lexical impoverishment as part of the process of language death. Paper presented at a linguistics seminar, SOAS, London, 1 October 2003.

Williamson, K. and Blench, R. (2000) Niger-Congo. In B. Heine and D. Nurse (eds) *African Languages: An Introduction* (pp. 11–42). Cambridge: Cambridge University Press.

Winter, J.C. (1976) Language shift among the Aasax, a hunter-gatherer tribe in Tanzania. *Sprache und Geschichte in Afrika (SUGIA)* 1, 175–204.

Wolff, E.H. (2000) Language and society. In B. Heine and D. Nurse (eds) *African Languages: An Introduction* (pp. 298–347). Cambridge: Cambridge University Press.

Wurm, S.A. (1996) *Atlas of the World Languages in Danger of Disappearing*. Paris: UNESCO.

Appendix 1: Nationally and Areally Dominant Languages of Africa, by Country

Country & number of languages	Nationally dominant languages	Areally dominant languages	
		Major	Minor
Algeria (15)	Arabic	Kabyle	Chaouia
Angola (39)	—	Umbundu, Kimbundu (Luanda), Kikongo	Chokwe, Shikwanyama, Luchazi, Luvale, Nyemba, Chimbunda, Shimbwera, Nkhumbi, Lunyaneka
Benin (48)	—	Fon-Gbe, Hausa, Yoruba, Bariba	Aja-Gbe, Ayizo-Gbe, Ditammari, Fulfude, Gen-Gbe, Gun-Gbe, Nago, Waci-Gbe
Botswana (28)	Setswana	Ikalanga	Shekgalagari, Naro
Burkina Faso (55)	Mossi-More	Dyula, Fulfude, Gurmanche	Bissa, Bwamu, Dagara, Nuni, Lobi, Lyele, Marka, Bobo Madare, Dogon, Songhay, Kasem, Koromfe, Samo
Burundi (3)	Kirundi	—	—
Cameroon (274)	—	Pidgin English, Fulfude, Ewondo (Bulu),	Bamun, Basaa, Fefe-Bamileke, Ghomala (Banjun), Kom (Bikom), Mafa, Masana, Medumba (Gabangte), Lamnso, Tupuri, Ngiemboon,

138

Country & number of languages	Nationally dominant languages	Areally dominant languages	
		Major	*Minor*
Cameroon (cont.)		Duala	Akouse, Bafia, Bafut, Bokoto, Eton, Fang, Gbaya, Gidar, Kanuri, Kenyang, Limbum, Makaa, Mmen, Musgu, Ngwe, Ngemba, Ngomba, Yemba
Canary Islands (2)	Spanish	—	—
Cape Verde (2)	Kabuverdi-anu	—	—
Central African Republic (53)	Sango	Gbaya, Banda	Manza, Bokoto, Fulfude, Yakoma, Gbanu, Kaba, Kare, Mbaka Ma'bo, Pana
Chad (126)	—	Arabic, Sara, Ngambay	Dazaga, Fulfude, Gulay, Kanembu, Kanuri, Maba, Marba, Masana, Mundang, Musey, Naba, Budura, Day, Gor, Laka, Mango, Masalit, Nancere
Comoro Islands (6)	Comorian (Shingazidja)	—	Shimaore, Shindzwani
Congo Republic (53)	Monokotuba (Kikongo)	Lingala	Kunyi, Punu, Teke, Mbosi, Lobala, Likwala
Côte d'Ivoire (58)	—	Anyi-Baule, Dyula, Senoufo	Abe, Attie, Dan, Dida, Guro, Lobi, Mahou, Abron, Bete, Kulango, Adyukru, Soninke
DRC (209)	—	Lingala, Kikongo, Kiswahili, Kiluba	Alur, Bembe, Ebuja, Chokwe, Fuliira, Kihunde, Kanyok, Kikomo, Ngbaka, Lunda (Ruund), Kisanga, Kilega,

Country & number of languages	Nationally dominant languages	Areally dominant languages	
		Major	Minor
DRC (cont.)		(Luba-Katanga)	Lendu, Logo, Tetela Mangbetu, Mbala, Kinandi, Mongo-Nkundu, Ngando, Kinyarwanda, Mashi, Taabwa (Rungu), Zande, Chibemba, Budu, Bwa, Ikela, Lugbara, Kisonge
Djibouti (4)	Afar	Somali	
Egypt (6)	Arabic	—	Domari, Bedawi
Equatorial Guinea (13)	Fang	—	Bube
Eritrea (11)	—	Tingrinya, Tigre	Afar, Bedawi, Kunama, Saho
Ethiopia (78)	Amharic	Oromo, Tigrinya, Somali	Afar, Gamo-Gofa-Awro, Gedeo (Derese), Gurage, Hadiyya, Kaficho (Kafa), Kambaata, Sidamo, Wolaytta
Gabon (40)	—	Fang	Mbere (Mbete), Omyene, Njembi, Punu, Teke
Gambia (9)	—	Mandinka (Malinke)	Fulfude, Wolof
Ghana (76)	—	Akan, Ewe, Dagbane, Ga/Adangme	Abron, Anyin, Dagaare, Nzema, Sehwi, Frafra, Gonja, Kasem, Konkomba, Mampruli, Kusaal (Kusale), Buli, Sisaala
Guinea (23)	—	Fulfude (Futa- Jalon), Mandinka (Malinke), Susu	Kissi, Kpelle, Dan, Mano, Loma, Yalunka, Kuranko

Country & number of languages	Nationally dominant languages	Areally dominant languages	
		Major	*Minor*
Guinea-Bissau (20)	Crioulo	Balanta, Fulfude	Mandinka (Malinke), Manjaca, Papel, Mankanya
Kenya (56)	Kiswahili	Gikuyu, Luo, Kikamba, Luyia	Bukusu, Embu, Giryama, Gusii, Kalenjin, Maasai, Meru, Somali
Lesotho (2)	Sesotho	—	—
Liberia (23)	—	Pidgin English, Kpelle, Bassa	Dan, Kisi, Klao, Mano
Libya (7)	Arabic	—	Nafusi, Domari
Madagascar (4)	Malagasy	—	Bushi
Malawi (39)	Chichewa (Chinyanja)	Chiyao, Chitumbuka	Elomwe, Nyakyusa (Ngonde), Chisena, Chitonga
Mali (28)	Bambara	Songhay, Soninke, Senoufo, Fulfude	Malinke, Arabic, Bozo, Dogon, Tamasheq, Xasonga, Bomu
Mauritania (6)	Hassaniyya (Arabic)	—	Fulfude
Mauritius (6)	Morisyen (Creole)	Bhojpari	Hindi
Mayotte (4)	Shimaore	—	Bushi
Morocco (7)	Arabic	—	—
Mozambique (33)	—	Emakhuwa (incl. Elomwe, Chuabo)	Shichopi, Makonde, Marenje, Chindau, Chinyanja, Shironga, Shisena

Country & number of languages	Nationally dominant languages	Areally dominant languages	
		Major	*Minor*
Namibia (26)	Afrikaans	Owambo, (incl. Oshindonga, Oshikwan-yama)	Nama, Rukwangali, Otjiherero
Niger (13)	Hausa	Zarma (Djerma)	Fulfude, Tamajaq (Tamashek), Kanuri, Songhay
Nigeria (485)	—	Hausa, Yoruba, Igbo	Araang, Ebira, Efik, Fulfude, Gbagyi, Isekiri, Mumunye, Ngas, Tiv, Urhobo, Ibibo, Idoma, Igala, Izon, Kanuri, Bade, Birom, Bura, (Pabir), Edo (Benin), Ekit, Esan, Gban, Gera, Goemai, Isoko, Tarok, Igede, Ikwere, Jju, Kirike, Ogbia, Bokyi, Bole, Bacama, Bariba, Bata, Bokyi, Eggon, Gun-Gbe, Kame, Mwangavul, Huba, Nigerian Pidgin
Réunion (3)	Réunion Creole	—	—
Rwanda (3)	Kinyarwanda	—	—
São Tomé è Principe (4)	Saotomense	—	—
Senegal (34)	Wolof	Fulfude, Serer-Sine	Jola-Fogny, Malinke (Mandinka), Soninke
Seychelles (3)	Seselwa	—	—
Sierra Leone (22)	Krio		Futa-Jalon (Fulfude), Kono, Sherbro, Kuranko, Limba, Loko, Susu

Country & number of languages	Nationally dominant languages	Areally dominant languages	
		Major	Minor
South Africa (23)	—	IsiZulu, IsiXhosa, Afrikaans, Sesotho, Setswana	Sepedi, Shitsonga, Tshivenda, Sindebele, Siswati
Sudan (121)	—	Arabic, Dinka	Bedani, Nuer, Bari, Massalit, Otuho, Shilluk, Toposa, Fur, Hausa, Kanuri, Nobiin, Kenuzi-Dongola, Zaghawa, Zande, Ama, Anuak, Didinga, Fulfude, Katcha-Kadugli-Miri, Luwo, Moru, Murle
Swaziland (4)	Siswati	—	—
Tanzania (124)	Kiswahili	Shisukuma	Chigogo, Oruhaya, Chimakonde, Kibena, Shichagga, Giha, Kihehe, Dholuo, Maasai, Kinyamwezi, Kibena, Lugulu, Kishambala, Chitumbuka, Kinyaturu (Rimi), Ichifipa, Makhuwa, Ikinyakyusa, Chiyao
Togo (42)	—	Kabiye, Ewe	Akposo, Gen-Gbe, Gourna, Waci-Gbe, Moba, Losu, Tem, Fulfude, Ntcham (Bassai)
Tunisia (4)	Arabic	—	—
Uganda (34)	—	Luganda, Kiswahili	Acholi, Alur, Lugbara, Ruchiga/Runyamkole, Lusoga, Rutooro/Runyoro, Lukenyi, Rukonjo, Lango, Lumasaaba, Teso

Country & number of languages	Nationally dominant languages	Areally dominant languages	
		Major	Minor
Zambia (38)	—	Chibemba, Chinyanja, Chitonga	Chikaonde, Lala-Bisa, Silozi, Ichilamba, Chilenje, Chilumba, Luvale, Mambwe-Lungu, Chinamwanga, Chinsenga, Ishinyiha, Chitumbuka
Zimbabwe (17)	Chishona	Sindebele	Chimanyika, Chinyanja, Chikalanga, Chindau, Chitonga

Appendix 2: Highly Endangered and Extinct or Nearly Extinct Languages of Africa, by Country

Country or territory	Highly endangered languages	Extinct or nearly extinct languages
Algeria	Tamacine-Tamazighe, Tidikelt–Tamazighe, Korandje	None
Angola	Nyendo, Kung-Koka, Maligo, !o!'Kung	Kwadi, Kwisi
Benin	Aguna, Basa, Boulba, Anii (Gisida), Anufo (Chokosi)	Tyanda
Botswana	Kua, Shua, Tshwa, ǀGwi, ǁGana, ǂKx'auǁ'ein, ǂHua; some of the varieties of Khwedam, namely: ǁAni, ǀAnda and Buga, Shiyeyi, Sebirwa, Setswapong	Deti-khwe, Gabake-Ntshori, Otjiherero of south Botswana
Burkina Faso	Ble, Khe, (Kheso), Khisa (Komono), Natioro, Sininkere (Silunde), Tiefo, Wara, Zarma	Noumoudara-Koumoudam (a dialect of Tiefo), Jelkuna
Burundi	None	None
Cameroon	Akum, Bakole, Bangandu, Barombi, Bati (Batiba Ngong), Bubia (Bobe),	Bikya, Bishuo, Bung, Busuu, Duli, Gey (Gueve), Nagumi (Bama), Ndai,

Country or territory	Highly endangered languages	Extinct or nearly extinct languages
Cameroon (cont.)	Buduma, Dimbong, Eman, Evant, Gyele, Hijuk, Isu, Kendem, Kolbila, Mampai, To, Tuotamb, Twendi, Yukuberi, Zizilivakan	Ngang, Yeni, Zumaya, Luo, Galke, Homa, Isuwu, Kole, Mboa, Mbong, Befon, Bonek, Ehobe, Poko
Canary Islands	None	Guanche
Cape Verde	None	None
CAR	Ali, Geme	Bodo, Birri
Chad	Barein, Boor (Bowara, Damraw), Fania (Mara, Kobe), Fongoro, Koke, Kindeje (Yaali), Kujange, Laal, Mawa (Mahoura), Miltu, Saba, Sokoro, Tamki, Tunia (Tounia, Tunya), Zan Gula (Moriil)	Berakou, Buso (Dam de Bouso), Gourdo, Horo (Hor), Massalat, Muskum, Niellim, Sokoro, Noy, Amdang, Ndam, Sarwa
Comoro Islands	Shindzwani, Shimaore (varieties of Shingazidja)	None
Congo Republic	Teke	Barambu, Boguru, Mangbele, Fumu, Ngbinda
Côte d'Ivoire	Beti (Eotile), Daho-Doo, Ega (Dies), Kodia (Kwadya)	Esuma, Dungi, Ligbi
DRC	Beeke (Beke), Bolondo, Bomboli, Gbanziri, Kwami (Khwami), Lonzo, Monzombo Yango (Gbendere), Dzando	Dongoko, Kazibati, Mampoko, Mbondo, Mongoba, Ngbee
Djibouti	None	None
Egypt	Kenuzi-Dongola, of Nubian	Coptic, Geez

Country or territory	Highly endangered languages	Extinct or nearly extinct languages
Egypt (cont.)	origin, and Sini (Siwa), of Berber origin	
Equatorial Guinea	None	None
Eritrea	Bilen (Bogo, Bileng)	Geez (Ancient Ethiopic)
Ethiopia	Anfillo, Bambassi, Kano, Kwama (Gongwama), Ometo, Saho, Opuuo (Cita, Kwira), Seze, Zay (Lak'í)	Argobba, Bayso, Burji, Gafat, Ganza (Ganzo, Koma), Rer Bare (Berebere, Adona), Agaw (western variety), Weyto, Kwegu (Bacha, Menja), Birale (Angota), Gatame, Ganjule, Qwarenya, Gomba, Kimanteney (Quara), K'emant Shabo, Omo-Murle, Xamtang'a, Geez
Gabon	Kande (Kanda), Pinji, Seki (Sekiani), Simba	None
Gambia	Kalanke	None
Ghana	Chakali, Chala, Dompo (Dumpo, Ndambo), Dwang, Hanga, Kamara, Kantosi, Nchumbulu	Boro
Guinea	Baga Binari, Baga Mandun, Baga Mtoteni	Baga Kaloum, Baga Koga, Baga Sobane (Burka, Sobane)
Guinea-Bissau	Badjara, Kasanga (Cassanga, Haal), Kobiana	Buy
Kenya	Boni, Dahalo, Burji (Bambala), Daasanach, Digo, Konkani (Goanese),	Elmolo (El Molo), Okiek (Akiek, Ndorobo), Yaaku (Mukodogo, Ndorobo),

Country or territory	Highly endangered languages	Extinct or nearly extinct languages
Kenya (cont.)	Malakote (Ilwana), Nubi (Kinubi), Sagalla (Teri), Sanye, Suba, Chifundi and Vumba (last two are Kiswahili dialects)	Omotik (Laamot, Ndorobo), Kore, Bong'om, Degere, Kinare, Lorkoti, Segeju, Sogoo, Ware
Lesotho	None	Seroa
Liberia	Gbii, Dewoin (Dey)	None
Libya	Awjilah (Augila), Domari, Ghadames	Sawkrah (Sokna)
Madagascar	None	None
Malawi	Malawian Ngoni	None
Mali	Bankagoma (Banka), Pana (Sama), Samoma	Jahanka (related to Soninke), Azer, Kakolo
Mauritania	Imeraguen (variety of Hassaniyya), Zenaga	None
Mauritius	None	None
Mayotte	Kiswahili	None
Morocco	None	Ghomara, Senhaja de Srair (Sanhaja of Srair)
Mozambique	Tekela (Mozambican Siswati), Sunda (Mozambican Zulu), Shichopi	None
Namibia	!Akhoe (‡Kx'au‖'ein), Kung-Ekoka (Kung), Hai‖'om, Mashi, Shiyeyi	‡Khomani and !Ora (Kora)
Niger	None	None
Nigeria	Abon (Abong, Ba'ban), Ahan (Ahaan), Ake (Akye),	Ajawa (Aja, Ajanci), Basa-Gumna (Basa-Kaduna,

Country or territory	Highly endangered languages	Extinct or nearly extinct languages
Nigeria (cont.)	Alege (Alegi, Uge, Ugbe), Ambo, Bali (Bibaali, Maya), Beele (Bele, Bellawa, Bina (Bogana, Binawa), Bure (Bubure), Buru, Cara (Caara, Nfachara), Ciwaga, Cori (Chori), Daba (Dabba), Defaka (Afakani), Dendi (Dandawa), Doka, Duhwa (Karfa, Kerifa, Nzuhwi), Dulbu, Dungu, (Dungi, Dunjawa), Dwai (Enji, Eastern Bode), Eruwa (Erohwa, Erakwa), Fam, Firan (Faran, Foron), Fungwa (Tufungwa, Ura, Ula), Gyem (Gyemawa, Gema), Hasha (Yashi), Horom, Hungworo (Ngwoi, Nkwoi, Ingwe), Idon, Iyive (Uive, Ndir, Asumbo), Janji (Anafejanzi, Jijanji), Jilbe (Zoulbou), Jimi (Bi-Gimu), Ju, Kaivi (Kaibi), Kariya (Kauyawa), Kiphawa (Vinahe, Wihe), Kinuhu (Kinuka), Korenoem (Kanam), Kono (Kowono), Kubi (Kuba, Kubawa), Kugbo, Kutto (Kupto), Kuturmi (Ada), Luri, Maghdi (Tala, Widala), Mala (Rumaya, Tumala), Mangas, Mashi, Mbogno (Kakaba,	Basa-Kuta), Bete, Centum (Cen Tum), Auyokama, Bade, Bassa-Kantagora, Faliof, Baissa, Gana, Holma (Da Holmaci, Bali Holma), Kiong (Akayon, Akoiyang, Iyoniyong), Bissaula, Lere, Lufu, Mawa, Njerep (Njerup), Odut, Putai (Margli West), Sheni (Shani, Shaiwi), Kpan, Kpati, Shaa, Taura, Tesherawa, Ziriya, Agara'iwa, Cena, Chamo, Gamo, Gubi, Gwara, Izora, Kiballo, Kir, Kudu, Nimbari, Ningi, Pishi, Shanga, Shau, Shirawa, Taura, Tijanji and Yashi

Country or territory	Highly endangered languages	Extinct or nearly extinct languages
Nigeria (cont.)	Kamkam), Mingang Doso (Munga Doso), Mundat, Mvanip (Magu), Ndunda, Nggwahyi, Ningye, Nkukoli (Lokoli, Ekuri), Piti (Pitti, Abisi), Ruma (Ruruma, Bagwama), Sha, Shiki (Gubi, Guba, Mashiki), Shuwa-Zamani (Kuzamani, Rishuwa, Kauru), Somyiwe (Kila), Surubu (Fiti), Tala, Tha (Joole Marga, Kapawa), Tumi (Tutumi, Kitimi, Vono (Kiwollo), Wase (Jukun Wase), Yangkam (Yankam, Basharawa, Bashar), Zangwal (Zwangal, Twar)	
Réunion	None	None
Rwanda	None	None
São Tomé è Principe	None	None
Senegal	Bandjana (Badyara, Pajadinka, Gola), Bainouk-Samik, Kobiana (Uboi, Buy)	Bedik, Haal
Seychelles	None	None
Sierra Leone	Bom (Bome, Bomo), Krim (Kim, Kiltim, Kirim, Kimi)	Bullom So (Bolem), Banta, Dama
Somalia	Chimiini (Bravanese), Bajuni (both remote varieties of Kiswahili), Garre (Af-Garre), Mushungulu,	Boni (Boon, Af-Boon), still spoken in Kenya

Country or territory	Highly endangered languages	Extinct or nearly extinct languages
Somalia (cont.)	Mmushungulu), Tunni (Af-Tunni)	
South Africa	Camtho (IsiCamtho), Sebowa, Gail, Kxoe (Mbarahuesa, Mbara-kwengo), Sebirwa	Korana (!Ora, !Kora), N/u, |Xam, ||Xegwi, Xiri (Criqua, Cape Hottentot), Ng'huki, Seroa, Gemsbok Nama
Sudan	Aja (Ajja, Adja), Aka, Bai (Bari), Baygo (Baigo, Bego), Boguru, Dair (Daier, Thaminyi), El Hugeirat, Logol (Lukfa), Logorik (Liguri), Mangayat (Mangaya, Bug), Mo'da (Gberi, Gweri, Muda), Molo (Malkan, Tara-ka-Molo), Njalgulgule (Nyolge, Bege, Beko), Nyamusa-molo, Suri (Surma), Talodi (Gajo-Mang, Jomang), Tese (Teis-umm-Danab, Keiga, Jirru), Tima (Lomorik, Lomuriki, Tama nik, Yibwa), Wali (Walari, Walarishe), Warnang (Werni)	Berti, Gule (Anej, Hamej, Fecakomoliyo), Homa, Togoyo (Togoy), Torona, Birked, Fongoro, Jur Modo, Kello, Mittu, Morokodo, Birgid, Bodo, Buga, Eliri, Haraza, Kidie, Lafofa, Kreish, Meroitic, Ngbinda, Tagbu, Tenet, Wetu
Swaziland	None	None
Tanzania	Daiso (Dhaiso), Gweno (Kigweno), Hadza (Hadzapi, Kitindiga), Akie (Ndorobo, Kisankara), Kwavi (Parakuyo), Bondei,	Aasax (Asax, Asak), Ongamo (Ngasa) Kikae (Old Kimakunduchi), Kwadza, Degere, Yeke, Hamba, Bahi, Ware

Country or territory	Highly endangered languages	Extinct or nearly extinct languages
Tanzania (cont.)	Doe, Burunge, Gorowa, Holoholo, Ikizu, Ikoma, Isanzu, Jiji, Kabwa, Kami, Kisi, Makwe, Manda, Mbungwe, Segeju (Sageju), Nghwele, Pimbwe, Rungwa, Suba, Alagwa (Wasi, Asi), Vidunda, Vinza, Zinza, Surwa, Sweta, Wanda, Zalamo (Zaramo)	
Togo	Sola (Soruba, Biyobe, Solamba), Kpesi, Igo (Ago, Ahonlan), Bissa, Bago	None
Tunisia	None	Sened (a Berber language), Sabir (a Petit Mauresque port Pidgin)
Uganda	Ik (Ngulak), Soo (So, Tepes)	Nyang'i (Nyangeya, Nyangia), Singa (Lusinga), Kooki, Napore
Zambia	Mbowe (Esimbowe), Yauma	Zambian varieties of Kxoe (now known as Khwedam in its grouping with other related languages)
Zimbabwe	Hiechware (Tshwa) and Dombe (Grimes, 2000)	None

Appendix 3: Number of Dominant and Minority Languages of Africa, by Country

Note that, since a number of languages are spoken in several countries, the total given at the end of the table comes to 2477. The actual number of African languages according to our survey is 2193. Similarly, the total for the languages of wider communication (LWC) is a simple sum of the figures in the last column. There are in fact seven LWC.

Country	No. of langs	Natl level	Dominant Areal level Major	Minor	Minority Highly endang'd	(Nearly) extinct	Less endang'd	LWC
Algeria	15	1	1	1	4	0	7	1
Angola	39	0	3	9	4	2	22	1
Benin	48	0	4	8	5	1	30	1
Botswana	28	1	1	2	16	2	7	1
Burkina Faso	55	1	3	14	8	2	29	1
Burundi	3	1	0	0	0	0	1	1
Cameroon	274	0	4	30	21	22	214	2
Canary Islands	2	1	0	0	0	1	0	0
Cape Verde	2	1	0	0	0	0	0	1
Cent. Afr. Rep.	53	1	2	10	2	2	37	1
Chad	126	0	3	18	14	13	90	1
Comoro Islands	6	1	0	0	2	0	1	2
Congo Republic	53	1	1	6	1	5	43	1

Country	No. of langs	Natl level	Dominant Areal level Major	Dominant Areal level Minor	Minority Highly endang'd	Minority (Nearly) extinct	Minority Less endang'd	LWC
Côte d'Ivoire	58	0	3	12	4	4	38	1
DRC	209	0	4	31	9	1	164	1
Djibouti	4	1	1	0	0	0	1	1
Egypt	6	1	0	2	2	2	1	0
Equat. Guinea	13	1	0	1	0	0	10	1
Eritrea	11	0	2	4	1	1	5	2
Ethiopia	78	1	3	9	9	19	55	1
Gabon	40	0	1	5	4	0	29	1
Gambia	9	0	1	2	1	0	4	1
Ghana	76	0	4	13	8	0	50	1
Guinea	23	0	3	7	3	3	9	1
Guinea-Bissau	20	1	2	4	3	1	13	1
Kenya	56	1	4	8	12	12	30	1
Lesotho	2	1	0	0	0	1	0	1
Liberia	23	0	3	4	2	0	13	1
Libya	7	1	0	2	3	1	1	0
Madagascar	4	1	0	0	0	0	2	1
Malawi	39	1	2	5	1	0	29	1
Mali	28	1	4	7	3	1	12	1
Mauritania	6	1	0	1	2	0	1	1
Mauritius	6	1	1	0	0	0	2	2
Mayotte	4	1	0	0	1	0	1	1
Morocco	7	1	0	0	0	2	5	1
Mozambique	33	0	2	6	3	0	21	1
Namibia	26	0	2	3	5	2	14	2
Niger	13	1	1	4	2	0	4	1

Country	No. of langs	Natl level	Dominant		Minority			LWC
			Areal level					
			Major	Minor	Highly endang'd	(Nearly) extinct	Less endang'd	
Nigeria	485	0	3	45	73	55	363	1
Reunion	3	1	0	0	0	0	1	1
Rwanda	3	1	0	0	0	0	1	1
São Tomé è Principe	4	1	0	0	1	0	1	1
Senegal	34	1	2	3	3	0	24	1
Seychelles	3	1	0	0	0	0	0	2
Sierra Leone	22	1	2	7	2	0	9	1
Somalia	12	1	0	1	5	1	3	2
South Africa	23	0	5	5	2	9	10	1
Sudan	121	0	2	23	23	23	72	1
Swaziland	4	1	0	0	0	0	2	1
Tanzania	124	1	1	19	33	9	69	1
Togo	42	0	2	9	5	0	25	1
Tunisia	4	1	0	0	0	2	2	1
Uganda	34	0	2	11	2	4	18	1
Zambia	38	0	3	12	2	1	20	1
Zimbabwe	17	1	1	5	2	1	7	1
Total	**2,477**	**36**	**88**	**370**	**308**	**201**	**1,623**	**50**

Index

Subjects and Authors

Languages